Eschatology

Eric M. Vail

THE FOUNDRY

PUBLISHING

Cover design: Arthur Cherry
Interior design: Sharon Page

Library of Congress Cataloging-in-Publication Data
Names: Vail, Eric M., author.
Title: Eschatology / Eric M. Vail.
Description: Kansas City, MO : The Foundry Publishing, 2020. | Series: The Wesleyan theology series | Includes bibliographical references. |
Summary: "Eric M. Vail explores in Eschatology the classic beliefs of Christianity by taking readers into Scripture and the teaching of the apostles. Readers will examine God's intentions for creation across the biblical narrative and consider how God works to fulfill those intentions. Vail brings Christianity's historic beliefs about the future of the world into focus. Ultimately, God is faithful and will bring creation into the fullness of what God has intended from the beginning"—Provided by publisher.
Identifiers: LCCN 2020022346 (print) | LCCN 2020022347 (ebook) | ISBN 9780834139671 | ISBN 9780834139688 (ebook)
Subjects: LCSH: Eschatology.
Classification: LCC BT821.3 .V345 2020 (print) | LCC BT821.3 (ebook) | DDC 236—dc23
LC record available at https://lccn.loc.gov/2020022346
LC ebook record available at https://lccn.loc.gov/2020022347

The internet addresses, email addresses, and phone numbers in this book are accurate at the time of publication. They are provided as a resource. The Foundry Publishing does not endorse them or vouch for their content or permanence.

10 9 8 7 6 5 4 3 2 1

Praise be to the God and Father of our Lord Jesus Christ, who has blessed us in the heavenly realms with every spiritual blessing in Christ. For he chose us in him before the creation of the world to be holy and blameless in his sight. In love he predestined us for adoption to sonship through Jesus Christ, in accordance with his pleasure and will—to the praise of his glorious grace, which he has freely given us in the One he loves. In him we have redemption through his blood, the forgiveness of sins, in accordance with the riches of God's grace that he lavished on us. With all wisdom and understanding, he made known to us the mystery of his will according to his good pleasure, which he purposed in Christ, to be put into effect when the times reach their fulfillment—to bring unity to all things in heaven and on earth under Christ.

Ephesians 1:3–10

Contents

Acknowledgments

1. Introducing Parameters
2. Background Check
3. The Narrative's Arc
4. Making All Things New
5. The Resurrection of the Dead
6. The Life to Follow
7. Heeding Revelation Today
8. Bearing Faithful Witness

Bibliography

Acknowledgments

First, I want to thank Alex Varughese and Bonnie Perry for their initiative with this book series. Thanks to them as well for inviting me to be one of the writers and entrusting me with two complementary volumes that explore the everlasting love of God for the world. *Atonement and Salvation* explores God's saving and atoning work, and this volume explores the fulfillment of creation in the glory of God's love. I pray that each book in the series will be a helpful discipleship resource.

Second, I thank Rick Williamson, who graciously offered feedback on the first drafts of each chapter. He was a source of encouragement through the writing process and his insights as a biblical scholar sprinkled in extra flavor along the way. Additionally, I thank Jeanne Serrao and Mike VanZant for multiple break-room conversations about chapter six and biblical views about death and judgment.

Third, Alex Varughese and Al Truesdale have offered valuable feedback on each chapter. I appreciate the ways in which they push me in the writing process. My exchanges with them always enhance the quality of the end product. Audra Spiven was also very helpful in finalizing the text for publication.

Fourth, Mount Vernon Nazarene University has been a tremendous support to me in the writing process. The faculty development committee extended to me a research grant, during which I was able to complete a significant portion of the background reading and write several of the chapters. Jeanne Serrao also helped craft my teaching schedule for the spring of 2018 so I had blocks of time in my week to continue writing. I am thankful for the backing of my colleagues and the encouragement they have offered.

Fifth, I cannot thank my family enough for their encouragement and support through these processes. My wife and kids have cheered me on and accommodated the months this project has taken. I thank my parents for their encouragement and for their feedback after taking the manuscript on a test run. I know they, along with my church family, have been praying for me along the way.

Lastly, I must acknowledge my students at MVNU who have shown their passion for the topics in this book and have asked great questions over the last few years. They have pushed me toward further reading and reflection. Multiple times in the writing of this book I have remembered classroom conversations and the ways we have wrestled with biblical teachings. Thanks, students, for keeping these issues ever fresh in my mind.

ONE

Introducing Parameters

God is the one who began this good work in you, and I am certain that
he won't stop before it is complete on the day that Christ Jesus returns.
—Philippians 1:6, CEV

He who was seated on the throne said, "I am making everything new!"
—Revelation 21:5a

We hope. We yearn. We imagine.

We sense the dissonance between God's sevenfold delight in creation—"it was good"—and the countless circumstances that just ought not to be in God's world.[1] There is a gap between what should be and what is. Humanity, with disturbing ingenuity, dismantles itself and the world through sinful living. Death, without thought or feeling, is all too ready to punch craters in the life of the world. In all its complexities, God's good creation was meant to shine in God's love. What God has intended and worked for from the beginning too often is not manifest. Yet we long that it would be, and we believe that it will be.

---

1. See the seven mentions of "good" in reference to creation in Genesis 1:4, 10, 12, 18, 21, 25, and 31.

In my book *Atonement and Salvation* I outline God's saving activities to bring about life in the face of death. I define salvation itself as "the preservation or granting of life in the face of deadly or life-grinding circumstances."[2] Atonement is foundational to salvation. It is the reconciling work God is doing to bring us into right fellowship with God and neighbor. Only through atonement—being restored in the Lord—can creation enjoy abundant life: salvation.[3] That saving and atoning work of God takes place centrally in Christ. Some of the saving work *has been done*, some *is being done*, and some of it *is yet to be done*.[4] Creation *is being saved* and *is receiving* salvation (1 Cor. 1:18; 1 Pet. 1:9). Yet the fullness of salvation, the completion of that work, remains ahead of us. As the apostle Peter says: "Praise be to the God and Father of our Lord Jesus Christ! In his great mercy he *has given* us new birth into a living hope through the resurrection of Jesus Christ from the dead, and into an inheritance that can never perish, spoil or fade. This inheritance *is kept* in heaven for you, who through faith are shielded by God's power *until the coming of the salvation that is ready to be revealed in the last time*" (1 Pet. 1:3–5, emphases added).

This volume on eschatology is a companion to the one on atonement and salvation. This book is about the completion of creation's salvation and about creation living as God always intended from the foundation of the world. The completion of salvation is itself not the final purpose for God's creation. God did not make the world for the

---

2. Eric M. Vail, *Atonement and Salvation: The Extravagance of God's Love* (Kansas City, MO: Beacon Hill Press of Kansas City, 2016), 14. See also J. Richard Middleton, *A New Heaven and a New Earth: Reclaiming Biblical Eschatology* (Grand Rapids: Baker Academic, 2014), 78–79.

3. Vail, *Atonement and Salvation*, 15–16.

4. Vail, *Atonement and Salvation*, 16–17.

God did not make the world for the purpose of having something to save. Rather, salvation is on the way to, or for the sake of, God's intent.

purpose of having something to save. Rather, salvation is on the way to, or for the sake of, God's intent. Salvation will be completed, and all things will be set free and made new so that everything will live under the rule of God and "God may be all in all" (1 Cor. 15:28).

The ultimate destiny of creation has classically been expressed as *the glory of God*.[5] According to Brent Peterson, "To glorify is, literally, to have one's image shine and radiate from oneself."[6] If God's glory, or God being all in all, is creation's destiny, then God's love will shine out from every part of creation. Indeed, "God gifts God's own self to creation so that all creation can actively express itself in love for God and neighbor. All creation is intended to express itself in the character of God's own self-giving, other-nurturing love."[7] The glory of God always has been and always will be our destiny. No matter what dissonance we sense with our present circumstances, God—in all God's glory—is our surest hope, and the one toward whom it is right for our hearts to yearn and imaginations to run. In Christ, God is doing the work of reconciliation (atonement) and salvation, that creation may enjoy God's purpose for it: abundant, everlasting life in the glory of God.

What Is Eschatology?

In the study of the Christian faith, nearly every topical area has a technical name. We know that a word ending in *–ology* denotes "the study of" some particular topic. In Greek, that *–ology* suffix comes from the word *logos*, which

---

5. Thomas A. Noble, "The Mission of the Holy Trinity;" Brent D. Peterson, "What Is the Point of God's Mission?" in *Missio Dei: A Wesleyan Understanding*, edited by Keith Schwanz and Joseph Coleson (Kansas City, MO: Beacon Hill Press of Kansas City, 2011), 83, 120.

6. Peterson, "What Is the Point of God's Mission?" 120.

7. Vail, *Atonement and Salvation*, 25.

means "word" or "reasoning." So another way to see *-ology* suffixes is to understand them as "words about" or "reasonings about" particular topics. Eschatology, then, is the study of all matters that come at the end of history and the intentions God has for creation—because, in Greek, the word *eschatos* means "last," or "final." In other words, eschatology covers where God desires to take creation and what it will take to get there.

As we explore the teaching of Scripture on eschatology, we thankfully do not have to start from scratch. We can learn from the perspective of the early church, who first received the Christian faith and put the Bible together in the form we have today. From early on, Christians had confessions (or rules of faith) that formalized what counted as the *apostolic* Christian faith, which helped guide the church in understanding Scripture.[8] At the Council of Nicaea in AD 325 Christians from all over the Roman Empire came together in agreement on the writings that would be our Scriptures as well as the norm for faithfully reading them. The written confession that came out of that council is what we call the Nicene Creed. The Nicene Creed was reaffirmed, with some additional points of clarification added, at the Council of Constantinople in AD 381. (This is why the Nicene Creed is sometimes called the Nicene-Constantinopolitan Creed.)

There are several points in the Nicene Creed that summarize Christian expectations for what is to come. The resurrected and ascended Christ "will come again in glory to judge the living and the dead, and his kingdom will have no end." At the end we proclaim that we "look for the

---

8. "Apostolic" for the early church simply meant being faithful to the teachings of the earliest apostles—those who had been with Jesus and had passed on what they saw and heard.

resurrection of the dead, and the life of the world to come." It is worth noting a key term from this last phrase in the creed, as it was first communicated in Greek and Latin.[9] In Greek, the portion that is translated as "the life of the world to come" may also carry the sense of "the life of the coming age, world, or time" (see Eph. 1:21; Heb. 6:5).[10] When combined, the two quoted sections of the creed give the sense of God's kingdom coming forever, which inaugurates a new type of life in that *age* (*aiōn*). This life is for the very *world* into which God's kingdom is coming. This understanding gives the word *aiōn* (aeon) in the creed a combined sense of age, time, *and* world. As Hermann Sasse writes, "The sense of 'time or course of the world' can easily pass over into that of the 'world' itself so that αἰών [aeon] approximates closely to κόσμος [cosmos]."[11]

In the Bible there is the present age, world, time, and there is the one to come.[12] The present age, world, or time has a beginning and ending, while the coming course of the world is endless, eternal. Scripture not only has these two aeons—courses of the world—but the second aeon also does not wait for the first age to end before it begins its turn.[13] There is a period of overlap between the two ages.

---

9. Here are the two relevant sections of the creed in both Greek and Latin.

Greek: Καὶ πάλιν ἐρχόμενον μετὰ δόξης κρῖναι ζῶντας καὶ νεκρούς, οὗ τῆς βασιλείας οὐκ ἔσται τέλος. . . . Προσδοκῶ ἀνάστασιν νεκρῶν. Καὶ ζωὴν τοῦ μέλλοντος αἰῶνος. Ἀμήν.

Latin: *Et íterum ventúrus est cum glória, Iudicáre vivos et mórtuos, Cuius regni non erit finis. . . . Et expécto resurrectiónem mortuórum, Et vitam ventúri sǽculi. Amen.*

10. See Hermann Sasse, "αἰών, αἰώνιος," in G. Kittel, G. W. Bromiley, & G. Friedrich, eds., *Theological Dictionary of the New Testament*, vol. 1 (Grand Rapids: William B. Eerdmans Publishing Company, 1977), 202–7.

11. Sasse, "αἰών, αἰώνιος," 203; see also 206.

12. Sasse, "αἰών, αἰώνιος," 205.

13. Sasse, "αἰών, αἰώνιος," 206. The coming age "is no longer merely in the future. Believers are already redeemed from this present evil αἰών [aeon] (Gal. 1:4) and have tasted the powers of the future αἰών [aeon] (Heb. 6:5). If, according

The Son's incarnation means that the ending of the first age has begun; we have been in the end times of the first age for several thousand years now.[14] Also in Christ, the everlasting aeon has begun: "The time has come. . . . The kingdom of God has come near" (Mark 1:15). Here is another way to think about the overlap: "through Christ new creation is begun. This is a new kind of life where sin and death are no more. The new creation has already been opened in Christ, but the old reality of sin and death has not yet passed away entirely."[15] Given the context of the Nicene Creed and the range of meanings for *aiōn* (aeon), the common English translation "the life of the world to come" is appropriate. As in the Greek, the Latin affirms the "life of the coming age, course of affairs, or world" (*sǽculi*) when Christ returns in glory and inaugurates an unending reign.[16]

The first portion of the creed confesses that the Lord's Prayer will be fulfilled. When Christ returns to earth and reigns forevermore, then God's will, in a complete way, will "be done, on earth as it is in heaven" (Matt. 6:10). The second portion confesses that our physical bodies will be raised from the grave as Christ's was. We will participate in the unending life of the coming age, entirely under God's dominion.[17] Christians across the centuries and around the

---

to the teaching of Jewish and early Christian eschatology, the resurrection of the dead implies the transition from the one aeon to the other and the beginning of the new and eternal creation, the new aeon has begun already, though as yet concealed from the eyes of men, in and with the resurrection of Christ, inasmuch as this is the beginning of the general resurrection (1 Cor. 15:20, 23)" (207).

14. Irenaeus suggested in the second century that Christ's coming happened "at the end of the times." Irenaeus of Lyons, *The Demonstration of the Apostolic Preaching*, trans. Armitage Robinson (New York: The Macmillan Co., 1920), https://www.ccel.org/ccel/irenaeus/demonstr.iv.html.

15. Vail, *Atonement and Salvation*, 29.

16. See "*Saeculum*" in *Oxford Latin Dictionary*, ed. by P. G. W. Glare (New York: Oxford University Press, 1982).

17. The shortened confession in the Apostles' Creed has all of these elements, except for any mention of Christ's unending kingdom. Similarly, the Athanasian

world share this creed in common as the rule of Christian orthodoxy. This summary of apostolic Christianity is meant to govern all Christians' reading of the Scriptures.

Let us, then, clarify the framing claims about creation and its destiny that the Nicene Creed gives for Christianity. First, the creed is Trinitarian. God's triune nature will frame the way we understand all things coming together in the glory of God, which is the glory of the inseparably working Father, Son, and Holy Spirit.

Second, the triune God is declared to be the Creator, Savior, and Life Giver for the world. The activities of the divine Persons included in the creed are very much for the sake of the world—its existence, redemption, blessing, deliverance from death, judgment, forgiveness, guidance, and eternal life. Nowhere does the creed imply that God's triune work for creation is temporary, for this age only. God's activity is directed toward or for the sake of the world, which will bring God's eternal reign into the world. As the creed frames it, the physical world itself will not be abandoned in the end. In other words, God's good creation will ultimately be redeemed and fully come under the reign of God for eternity.

Third, God's creative and redemptive activities have never been for individual human beings only. From beginning to end God is taking the whole of creation into its intended life in the glory of God.[18]

Creed finishes: "He ascended into heaven, he sitteth at the right hand of the Father, God Almighty, from whence he will come to judge the quick and the dead. At whose coming all men will rise again with their bodies and shall give account for their own works. And they that have done good shall go into life everlasting; and they that have done evil into everlasting fire. This is the Catholic Faith, which except a man believe faithfully, he cannot be saved." The Athanasian Creed, http://anglicansonline.org/basics/athanasian.html.

18. See, for example, Vail, *Atonement and Salvation*, 31–62; J. Richard Middleton, *A New Heaven and a New Earth*; and Howard A. Snyder and Joel Scandrett,

Lastly, there are contrasting ways to understand that God has a purpose or intention for the world. On one hand, it could signal that God has a blueprint that has been fixed from the beginning and that God is orchestrating step-by-step processes preordained according to that plan. On the other hand, it could mean there is a manner in which God intends all things to share fellowship. Rather than conformity to a blueprint and building sequence, this latter understanding implies open-ended dialogue between God and creation—an unfolding journey of discovery.[19] This would be like desiring all your family members to get along at the family reunion without you needing to script every conversation and action. Since the creed does not specify which way to go on this issue, the Scriptures will have to be examined.

Outline for This Study

The Nicene Creed is the rule for true Christian belief. It is meant to summarize the witness of the Scriptures, as Jesus's own disciples explained them within the early church (Luke 24:27, 32; Acts 2:42; 8:35). This book is an exploration of the approaches to eschatology within Scripture. That will give us the foundation for the apostolic faith confessed among Christians.

The following chapter starts the exploration of Scripture by looking at the character of God and God's relationship with the world. Thus, we will be starting with the area

Salvation Means Creation Healed: The Ecology of Sin and Grace: Overcoming the Divorce between Earth and Heaven (Eugene, OR: Cascade Books, 2011).

19. See D. Lyle Dabney, "The Nature of the Spirit: Creation as a Premonition of God" in *The Work of the Spirit: Pneumatology and Pentecostalism,* edited by Michael Welker (Grand Rapids: William B. Eerdmans Publishing Company, 2006), 71–86.

of eschatology that reflects on God's purpose and intention for creation.

Chapter 3 will start to explore the other side of eschatology, which considers the unfolding processes that will get creation to its intended destiny—also thought of as "last things." If there is a singular *last thing* that is most central or key to them all, it is God dwelling with us. We will reflect on some of the implications that accompany the glory of God's presence.

Chapters 4, 5, and 6 work through major topics within eschatology—the life of the world to come, the resurrection of the dead, and what will become of righteous and wicked people. Each topic will be handled in its own chapter. I recommend reading them in order. Chapter 6, especially, assumes that readers will already have chapter 5 as background.

Next, the book of Revelation has so overshadowed people's imaginations about eschatology that chapter 7 is devoted to clarifying Revelation's central function and message. Revelation will factor into the topical explorations of earlier chapters. Nevertheless, the book itself needs its own space.

The final chapter, chapter 8, will explore a few points of contrast between the reading of Scripture presented in this book and trends that are circulating among Christians today.

At least one point can be clarified here at the beginning—the basis for our hope and comfort. The processes by which God will transform our present circumstances into the everlasting age have not always been clearly stated, or if they have been clearly stated, they have been more terrifying than good news. For both of these reasons, the topic of final things has not always been pleasant. We typically value clarity over ambiguity. In one of my college classes, I can only imagine my students' revolt if I gave this minimal instruction: *give me a report on the Christian faith.* It is not that my students are disrespectful or unwilling to work. Rather, the instruction lacks clarity. It says nothing about when the report is due, how long it should be, the medium of communication, how comprehensive to be, the intended audience, the criteria I will use for evaluating their work, and many other significant factors. Ambiguity raises anxiety levels for many people. No matter their driving motivation to perform, people want clarity about any game they are playing. What is the goal? And what are the rules? It seems reasonable for people to alleviate ambiguities in any area of life by seeking answers to their questions about what to do and how to do it. Certainly something as significant as creation's ultimate eternal destiny is no exception. Here, the stakes could not be any higher.

Fascination and terror consume many people on the topic of end times and ultimate destiny. With such high stakes and the discomfort that uncertainty brings, the pull toward knowing the future is strong. Some voices in Christian circles offer turn-by-turn roadmaps of what lies ahead—the exact roads we will travel, the length of time we will be on each one, and what experiences we will have along the way. These voices promise to alleviate our anxiety by offering clarity. However, they tend to conflict with each other on the details more often than they agree, leaving bystanders without the promised certainty. If this debate over details about the future does not perpetuate anxiety, the grim pictures painted about what lies ahead can move us toward outright fear. Who would find any comfort in a journey to the end that includes beastly creatures, widespread destruction and slaughter, and eternal torment?

There is hope and comfort that we can have today about the end times and ultimate destiny. However, it is not dependent on winning debates over who has the most accurate roadmap. This book does not offer a detailed traveler's guide to the future. Seeking certainty about future events is one approach toward assurance that relies on a deterministic picture of God's creation—its workings, purpose, and our way of marching to its end. However, there is an altogether different picture of God's creation and its destiny presented in this book.

The difference is not just a matter of quibbling over a detail of events here and there. It is as though there are two entirely different games being played. In the picture offered here, comfort and hope for the future are not found in uncovering and following a predetermined sequence of events. Rather, our whole life and destiny is from, in, and for the glory of our triune Creator. We are not securing our salvation or peace of mind based on details that may or may not happen in the history of the world. God is our sure foundation and hope; God's loving character, faithfulness, intentions, and capability give us comfort. Our trust and hope are in the Lord.

TWO

Background Check

When the men got up to leave, they looked down toward Sodom, and Abraham walked along with them to see them on their way. Then the LORD *said, "Shall I hide from Abraham what I am about to do?"*

—Genesis 18:16–17

How much background does it take to understand an event? One afternoon I came into the middle of a TV news story about a professional baseball game.[1] The first image I saw was a batter getting hit by a pitch. The batter then charged the pitcher on the mound, throwing wild punches. The only background I had for the batter's behavior was seeing him get hit with a 98-mph fastball. Eventually I caught from the newscaster that the pitcher likely aimed at the batter intentionally because of a grudge from their last faceoff two years prior. That gave background to both the pitcher's action and why the batter may have responded so explosively.

---

1. A written account of the event I saw on TV is given here: http://ftw .usatoday.com/2017/05/bryce-harper-throws-helmet-hunter-strickland-brawl -punch-video-giants-nationals-mlb-brawl-nationals-fight.

Yet is even this enough background to understand the event? Were there other factors involved? Perhaps the players were under heavy emotional pressure in their personal lives that added to their volatility that day. Maybe they were short on sleep, with lowered inhibitions. They could have been taught as children to treat opponents according to this code of violence, or they were prodded before the game toward this action by teammates or mentors. Even if all of these personal and social factors could be named, it still does not help us know what meaning to make of the information. There are differing frameworks that could be used to draw conclusions about the situation.

As the news commentator continued, he sounded complimentary of the batter. In his logic the batter chose the best course by punching the pitcher and then accepting a suspension from the league as punishment. The commentator saw that as positive: that somehow "justice" was being worked out against the pitcher and then the batter. From the commentator's perspective, this whole exchange was logical and ordered. But what if the event was *not* positive or just? What if it was entirely a display of sin—in both logic and action? The same data could be processed through a different framework, where a response of remorse and repentance would be appropriate. How far back do we need to go to make accurate sense of an event? Background details are important, and so is consideration of the framework we use for understanding the details.

In the area of eschatology it might feel natural to look forward toward the final events that will happen this side of eternity and start commenting on them. Yet how much background would those events require to understand them rightly? Certainly it would give an incomplete picture without any backstory to offer context. It would probably be important to know that God's good creation has been subjected to sin's corrupting effects and that God has been at work to redeem the world through Christ and will ultimately sort everything out. However, we could still give meaning to the pieces according to a logic that is flawed. The place where eschatology must start is not at the end but at the beginning. And it does not start with created things and their history but with the Creator. The triune God is the beginning and end of all things; God is the measure for discerning truth. The character and activity of God are the baseline for making sense of God's creation. Rather than starting with last things, eschatology starts with the One who is creation's Beginning and End—that is, with God and God's intentions for creation from the beginning.

The Purpose of Creation

We know who God is on the basis of God's self-revelation to us. This initiative on God's part shows that God intends to be known by and to share communion with creation. God is highly interactive with the world. God is continually engaged in giving life (Ps. 104:29–30; 1 Cor. 15:45); sharing in dialogue (Gen. 18); offering direction (Deut. 12:28; Ps. 119:105); saving (Ps. 40:1–2; Rev. 7:9–10); correcting through warning or discipline (2 Sam. 12; Heb. 12:5–11); and entering covenant bonds with God's own creation (Gen. 9:11, 15; Gen. 15, 17; Exod. 19–20; 1 Chron. 17; Luke 22:15–20). We could imagine having a deity who brought forth creation and remained utterly hidden or antisocial. However, from the very beginning, and all the way through, the living God connects with the world in a reciprocal manner. This type of interactive relationship appears to be God's own way of operating and God's intent for creation. There is also a certain character to the interactions between God and creation (and among creatures) that shows God's intentions. That character is the self-giving, other-nurturing love most clearly demonstrated in Christ laying down his life for the salvation of the world (1 John 3:16; 4:9–10).

While God is most clearly revealed in Christ, and God's ultimate intentions for the world come together in him (in the middle of the story), God's character and intentions for creation can be seen from the dawn of creation. The Bible begins with an impossibility for the world. "Now the earth was formless and empty" (Gen. 1:2).[2] The Hebrew word translated as "formless" is *tohu*. This is an "uncultivated wilderness," or "desert."[3] The other word, *bohu*, means "empty." A strict translation of this verse would be that the earth was "desert-like and empty" or "desolate and uninhabited."[4] This condition is never positive in Scripture.

Making a place a desert—whether it is Canaan or any other land—is a sign of judgment (see Isa. 14:17; 17:2, 9; Jer. 17:5–8; 50:10–13; Zeph. 2:4, 13; and Mal. 1:3). Indeed, the destruction of Babylon in Jeremiah 51:42–43 is described as a reversal of the creation processes depicted in Genesis 1:2–10. On the other hand, salvation in Isaiah 35:1–4 and Ezekiel 36:1–12 is painted as

---

2. There are some resources available to help us read the opening chapters of Genesis against the backdrop of their ancient Near Eastern context. On Genesis 1, see John H. Walton, *The Lost World of Genesis One: Ancient Cosmology and the Origins Debate* (Downers Grove, IL: InterVarsity Press, 2009); David Toshio Tsumura, *Creation and Destruction: A Reappraisal of the* Chaoskampf *Theory in the Old Testament* (Winona Lake, IN: Eisenbrauns, 2005). For a look at Genesis 1–11, see Richard S. Hess and David Toshio Tsumura, eds., *I Studied Inscriptions from before the Flood: Ancient Near Eastern, Literary, and Linguistic Approaches to Genesis 1–11*, Sources for Biblical and Theological Study, vol. 4 (Winona Lake, IN: Eisenbrauns, 1994). An easy starting point is a brief article by Joseph Lam, "Biblical Creation in its Ancient Near Eastern Context," *BioLogos* (April 21, 2010), http://biologos.org/uploads/projects/lam_scholarly_essay.pdf.

3. David Toshio Tsumura, *Creation and Destruction: A Reappraisal of the* Chaoskampf *Theory in the Old Testament* (Winona Lake, IN: Eisenbrauns, 2005), 33; see 9–35.

4. Vail, *Atonement and Salvation*, 23.

a progression from empty desert to fruitful land (see Isa. 40:3; 41:17–20; 42:5–17).[5]

Not only does Genesis 1 start with an empty wasteland, it is also entirely dark and buried under water.[6] No amount of waiting could ever increase the population of zero without God intervening with light, reorganization, cultivation, and enlivenment by God's Spirit. The first we hear of God in this primal circumstance is that God is present with the impossible: the Spirit of God hovers over the waters. God's presence and activity with creation is the necessary grace that will lead toward all life and abundance. By the Spirit, as God speaks, there is the possibility of response. God's first actions of creating light (v. 3), making space in the waters (vv. 6–7), and parting the waters so dry ground can appear (vv. 9–10) set the stage for God's and creation's interactions.

The grace of God's Spirit and Word invoke creation's responsiveness in ways that mirror God's own care. The waters are called to move aside for the benefit of the land (v. 9), and they are again called for the support of fish and birds (v. 20). The land is called upon to sustain vegetation (v. 11) and the life cycles of land creatures (v. 24). The lights in the sky are tasked with telling time through the ordering of days and seasons (v. 14). The vegetation and animals are to be productive, fill up the earth, and share in an interconnected relationship (vv. 12, 22, 29–30). Even the humans are given the task of benefiting the earth and its inhabitants

---

5. Vail, *Atonement and Salvation*, 144 (note 5).

6. Note the similarity between the starting condition of the waters over the land in Genesis 1:2–9 and Psalm 104:5–9, which says, "He set the earth on its foundations; it can never be moved. You covered it with the watery depths as with a garment; the waters stood above the mountains. But at your rebuke the waters fled, at the sound of your thunder they took to flight; they flowed over the mountains, they went down into the valleys, to the place you assigned for them. You set a boundary they cannot cross; never again will they cover the earth."

We are born out of divine, self-giving, other-nurturing love—with the intention of reflecting that same love.

(v. 28), without being given these things under their charge for consumption (vv. 29–30). Just as God does not operate in Genesis 1 for God's own sake, nothing God creates is created to operate for its own sake. Rather, all things are to operate for the sake of others and the vitality of the whole system. God's own self-outpouring through the Spirit and Word is to be mirrored by God's creation. Jesus's summary of all commandments as love for God and neighbor are not tasks added onto humankind or creation's intended life; they are a clarification of our own created identity. God's own love is at work as the very possibility for creation's existence and life. We are born out of divine, self-giving, other-nurturing love—with the intention of reflecting that same love. Our life looks like the Life Giver.

God's creating grace fosters a community of love that elicits a community of self-expression. God calls ("Let the waters," "Let the land") and blesses ("Be fruitful and multiply"). The enlivening grace of the Spirit and evoking Word prompt responsiveness from creation. If God's creation is going to image the love of its Creator, it must come alive with the type of personal agency that is necessary for being a lover of others. God makes a world with inhabitants that is blessed with the grace to act in loving agency, and it must give an account of itself for living contrary to what God empowers it to be. If God's primary attribute was God's sovereign will, then this would all be different; it would not only show up in *how* God creates but also in *what* God creates. God's unquestionable will would show up in God single-handedly doing everything, declaring reality without room for cooperative response, or in a puppet creation that is merely manifesting the workings of God's sovereign hand. This is, however, not the case in Genesis 1. In advance, the Spirit of God makes possible creation's responsiveness to the invocation from God's Word. As things move along,

God blesses creation's ongoing agency in moving toward the fulfillment of God's purposes for creation: abiding in and shining forth God's love.

Another example of the way our Scriptures teach about God's intention for creaturely agency is the garden of Eden narrative. Genesis 2:19–20 says, "Now the LORD God had formed out of the ground all the wild animals and all the birds in the sky. He brought them to the man to see what he would name them; and whatever the man called each living creature, that was its name. So the man gave names to all the livestock, the birds in the sky and all the wild animals." Human agency and ingenuity are demonstrated in the garden even before sin is present in the narrative. God's creation is meant to be expressive and active "in the naming—the shaping and ordering—of God's world."[7] This intention suggests that "meanings are not present or eternally determined in the mind of God."[8] There is a major difference in how God is understood, for example, in the Qur'an's version of the story. There, divine sovereignty is forefront. In the Qur'an "God teaches Adam the right names of each and every thing. . . . There is little if any room for human naming, for human interpretation and elaboration."[9] Every detail is according to a divine edict, straight out of the mind of God. The Hebrew and Christian Scriptures, however, teach that God opens up space for creation to speak its own word, and that words that are not God's have a rightful place in the goodness of God's creation.

The narratives of Scripture continue to reveal the way God interacts with humankind as they speak out. In the

---

7. Michael Lodahl, *Claiming Abraham: Reading the Bible and the Qur'an Side by Side* (Grand Rapids: Brazos Press, 2010), 96.

8. Lodahl, *Claiming Abraham*, 96.

9. Lodahl, *Claiming Abraham*, 96. See also the Qur'an 2.30–33.

account of Abraham and Sarah, God promised a child. They tried to bring about God's promise through their own means—their servant Hagar bore Ishmael (see Gen. 16). It was an understandable direction to go, since Sarah was so old (18:11). This first part of the story is a creaturely innovation that God did not embrace. God still gave Sarah her own son, Isaac, just as God promised. When Sarah gave birth to Isaac, she wanted Ishmael to leave so there would be no confusion about which child was the one God had promised (21:10). God accepted this solution from Sarah. It may not have been Abraham's preference (v. 11), nor did it demonstrate God's ultimate desire that humankind would perfectly love their neighbors as themselves without fear of injury. Nevertheless, God told Abraham that Sarah's wish should be obeyed; her voice should be included as God worked toward God's ultimate purposes (vv. 12–13). In addition, God was willing to bless and watch over Hagar and Ishmael in spite of Ishmael not being the child God promised to Abraham and Sarah (16:9–12; 21:12–20). God may not have condoned Abraham and Sarah's innovation of using Hagar to bear a descendant, but God still blessed Hagar and Ishmael bountifully.

In the interchange between God and creation, surely the Scriptures do not intend for us to picture God cringing at every expression of free agency—as if we always get it wrong. God was not wincing at every name Adam gave the animals. Sarah did not fall out of favor with God when she spoke up about what she wanted to have happen with a perceived threat. Creaturely agency is not a hurdle for God to overcome. It is not an imperfect feature of creation until God can establish a better arrangement. It is not a temporary detour to God getting us to conform to the exact blueprint God has in mind. God created us to have and keep our ingenuity and voice. While we know all creation is meant to express itself out of the self-giving, other-nurturing love of God with which God gifts us through the Spirit and Word, God's creative instructions are fairly open-ended: put forth fish, birds, vegetation, and land animals; separate, keep time, reproduce, and take care of the earth and fellow creatures. There is great room in all of that for wildly diverse and creative cooperation that reflects God's love. Certainly the Scriptures also name times when God gives specific instructions—leave your family and homeland (Gen. 12), go to Pharaoh (Exod. 3), anoint this person as king (1 Sam. 9; 16), marry Gomer (Hos. 1), and more. Nevertheless, for the vast majority of people and daily activity, there is no direct word from the Lord about the exact thing to do.

As one example, the two Hebrew midwives at the beginning of Exodus serve as the benchmark in the narrative for what it means to live life in the fear of the Lord (Exod. 1:15–21). There is no mention that God commanded them to disobey Pharaoh's order to kill every Hebrew boy upon delivery. But as people who feared the Lord, they had sense enough to know that their purpose in the world was to be life-fostering agents and not agents of death. They were capable of managing a course of action without a direct instruction from the Lord, and they were blessed for their faithfulness (vv. 20–21).

The apostle Paul is a second example. He did not have a precise word from the Lord on every issue as he tried to lead the early churches (1 Cor. 7:12, 25), but he gave guidance based on the character of what he did know. Perhaps this openness in life is why in Philippians 2 his approach was to lay out before the Philippian church what we know about Christ (vv. 4–11) and then tell them to work out collectively the way to proceed in their circumstances according to Christ's pattern (vv. 12–13). God gives life to a world where God does not have to dictate every detail in order for us all to interact in perfect love. By grace, all parts of creation can imaginatively contribute to what life in God's very good creation looks like.

It is difficult to visualize the balance of these two sides. On one hand, God's ultimate intention is that creation would have self-expression and be a chorus of voices that shape the ways our loving fellowship is borne out. On the other hand, life in the world has some God-given structure and is not a free-for-all. Genesis 1 already showed that the world did not just emerge willy-nilly without any divine direction whatsoever. There were at least basic parameters that there would be distinct spaces (land, sea, air), times (day, night, seasons), and functions for things. Within those parameters, however, particulars are not typically dictated.

In terms of the exact activities we are to do, Genesis 2 and 3 offer an image of healthy and unhealthy creaturely expression. God established a certain framework for life in Genesis 2 by creating a garden in which the humans would live. Of all the trees that grew up out of the ground, two were in "the middle of the garden" (v. 9) and had names. There was the tree of life and the tree of the knowledge of good and evil. These trees had a prominent function in God's design for garden living. We should not be thrown off that one of the trees had the word "evil" in its name. They both had God as their source and were God-intended features of the garden. It is common to view the tree of the knowledge of good and evil as a menacing object or as a carrot of temptation God dangled in front of the humans' noses. However, in God's arrangement, God plants both trees *together*. The tree of life is meant to be their food, and the tree of the knowledge of good and evil is supposed to be right there with it but never used for their sustenance.

What is the meaning of this arrangement? As Terence Fretheim notes, "the phrase 'good and evil' functions as an idiomatic expression in which the individual words do not have their normal meanings (hence the phrase does not speak to the question of the existence of evil; a knowledge of the 'good' is assumed from 2:9; 3:5)."[10] The phrase refers to something else. As in Genesis 2:9, "good and evil" appears with the verb "know" in Deuteronomy 1:39 and 2 Samuel 19:35.[11] We find clarification about the idiom's meaning from these other two places in the Old Testament where the same Hebrew wording appears, as well as from places where similar wording appears. Deuteronomy 1:39 says that young children do not yet have the knowledge of good and evil. Interpreters suggest that here the idea is equivalent to discernment or the ability to make sound choices (see also Isa. 7:15–16). Children have no sense of the ramifications of their actions. While not identical wording, 1 Kings 3:9 helps show this belief in Hebrew thinking. Solomon prayed with similar wording for the knowledge of good and evil at the dedication of the temple—or in the NIV, "a discerning heart to govern your people and to distinguish between right and wrong."[12] Solomon's request pleased God, and God gave him "a wise and discerning heart" (v. 12). Second Samuel 19:35 uses the wording of Genesis 2:9, and in it, an older man is losing the knowledge of good and evil.

In these other locations in the Old Testament, the idea behind the knowledge of good and evil points to

---

10. For a helpful treatment on how "good and evil" functions as an idiom in this passage and other passages in the Old Testament, see Terence E. Fretheim, "The Book of Genesis," in *The New Interpreter's Bible: Genesis to Leviticus*, Vol. 1 (Nashville: Abingdon Press, 1994), 350–51.

11. Fretheim, "The Book of Genesis," 351.

12. Fretheim, "The Book of Genesis," 351.

human discernment or wisdom. "For the writer, the key issue involves the discernment of what is in one's own best interests, not the fruit of the tree as fruit or any specific content of the knowledge or knowledge generally."[13] Children do not have discernment yet (Deut. 1:39); Solomon had it in abundance (1 Kings 3:12); and it may slip away late in life (2 Sam. 19:35). Discernment is a good feature for humankind to have if God is opening up space for us to make good contributions (like Adam naming the animals). Nevertheless, no matter how wise God made Solomon—"so that there will never have been anyone like you, nor will there ever be" (1 Kings 3:12)—Solomon was still to "walk in obedience to [God] and keep [God's] decrees and commands" (v. 14). Following God would give Solomon "a long life" (v. 14).

These passages explain the dynamic of the two trees in the perfection of God's garden. Humans were created to become wise and discerning creatures. Imagine the mess of God calling us to be loving contributors in the world without any sense to be able to do that well. That is as scary as everyone trying to drive cars with no system for steering! We would never get where we were supposed to go, and we would be in great danger in the meantime. God gives us discernment as a good feature of creation. But we are not to live off of that fruit of the knowledge of good and evil. That tree is to be planted right beside God's tree of life. And the fruit of our wisdom is not to be our sustenance. Only God and God's ways can and should feed us.[14] As Solomon

---

13. Fretheim, "The Book of Genesis," 351.

14. Victor Hamilton concludes, "What is forbidden to man is the power to decide for himself what is in his best interests and what is not. This is a decision God has not delegated to the earthling. . . . Man has indeed become a god whenever he makes his own self the center, the springboard, and the only frame of reference for moral guidelines." Victor P. Hamilton, *The Book of Genesis: Chapters 1-17*, New International Commentary on the Old Testament (Grand Rapids:

himself is credited with writing: "Trust in the LORD with all your heart and lean not on your own understanding; in all your ways submit to him, and he will make your paths straight" (Prov. 3:5-6). God is our source, our direction, and our end. God goes before us in hovering over the waters, in the pillar of cloud and fire, in the gift of the Torah, and in Jesus Christ and the Holy Spirit.

God does not have to spell out every detail of every task for us; the capacity to discern good and evil is part of the way God created us. We can navigate *within* the vision of life that God has revealed to us, as the Holy Spirit continually fans godly desire within our hearts. Our wisdom is to be put to living in the goodness of God instead of becoming a competing version of what the good life might be. Only God is *good*; and only creaturely expression that abides in the gifts of God's Son and Spirit will result in the joy of abundant, good life. Being our own god in making up what is good, according to our own desires (Phil. 3:19; 1 John. 2:15–17), leads to increased toil and ultimately death. In folly, we put our ingenuity toward going directions that are discordant with God's love. Those are *dead ends*.

Creation cannot be the source of its own life or destiny; only God can truly be our Creator, Sustainer, and End—our Alpha and Omega (Rev. 1:8; 21:6; 22:13). Creation trying to be its own life is like a battery-powered toy trying to say it will operate forever off of its finite batteries. Even if it has rechargeable batteries, the toy has no capacity within itself to charge those batteries. Trying to live off our own resources, as clever as we may be, not only results in death but also in a story of excessive toil and destruction on the way there.

William B. Eerdmans Publishing Company, 1990), 166. See also, concerning the trees in this narrative, Fretheim, "The Book of Genesis," 350–52, 361.

Implications for Eschatology

Eschatology deals with both the last things and the ultimate intentions God has for creation. It is hard to make sense of events without context. How can we make sense of the last things in this age and the age to come without knowing the trajectory of where we are coming from? It is also important to pay attention to God and God's intentions for creation across time.

The investigation in this chapter has shown God's love poured out for the benefit of the world. It has shown that the world itself is enlivened so it can likewise be expressive of that divine-like love toward God and neighbor. This is the tremendous gift of God to creation—that all things can live in the dynamics of shared love that God enjoys eternally as Father, Son, and Holy Spirit. Creation is brought forth out of God's outpoured love as the Spirit enables creation's responsiveness to the eliciting Word of God. The very foundation and purpose of all creaturely existence is to abide in God's outpoured love and be imaginative contributors to the shape of this community that embodies loving care for others. It is part of God's intention that creation would have its own voice in contributing to that shared life. Creation is meant to express itself in its own acts of God-enabled love. It does not have to speak a script that God has written out in precise detail; rather, the intention is for God and creation to go on a journey together of shared life within the beauty of God's love. Life in creation is meant to be an extemporaneous dance between Creator and creation, the common thread being loving reciprocity.

Life in the world does not unfold in a predestined sequence of events, nor is it micromanaged by divine dictate for every step. There is no map to decode. We do not know, nor can we figure out, when Christ will return (Matt. 24:42;

25:13); even the angels and the Son do not know (Matt. 24:36). Events (past, present, and future) have to be interpreted in a framework. We have all the hopes and promises of full salvation—the resurrection of our bodies along with all things being made new—and the coming age of the world. We have assurance in Christ that God will bring to fulfillment what God has started. Rather than figure out a predetermined future, we should already be living a foretaste of creation's future life—living faithfully in the glory of God's love toward God and our neighbor as ourselves. "Darkness gives way to [holiness's] beams of light as it pours itself on the hearts of men. Where holiness prevails is paradise restored, the impress of the divine image regained, the kingdom of heaven received, and human hearts filled with the light and glory of God."[15] As we cooperate in the sanctifying grace of God, we already participate in a preview of the coming age. The church is to be a living testament of creaturely life in the Lord that is a free, reciprocal, and loving fellowship.

Another way to talk about the life represented in the church is to say that, from beginning to end, "God's purpose is to call into being and find a dwelling place in the fellowship of a community that God self-gifts to enjoy the love God has in God's self as Father, Son, and Holy Spirit. In creating the heavens and the earth, God is creating a temple-dwelling place, to be with us and for us."[16] Into this life we have been made alive. For all this, we ought always to give our thanks to God. God our Father is the one from

---

15. F. E. Hill, "The Beauty of Holiness," *The Nazarene Messenger* 3:30 (December 21, 1899), 7.

16. Vail, "The Holiness Foundation of Mission," *Didache: Faithful Teaching* 13:1 (Summer 2013), 1, http://didache.nazarene.org/index.php/volume-13-1/894 -didache-v13n1-03-mission-vail1/file.

whom all these gifts flow[17] and the one toward whom all things are rightfully ordered and all praise due.[18]

> *Glory be to the Father, and to the Son, and to the Holy Ghost:*
> *As it was in the beginning, is now, and ever shall be,*
> *world without end. Amen.*[19]

---

17. See Rom. 1:7; 1 Cor. 1:3; 2 Cor. 1:2; Gal. 1:3–4; Eph. 1:2–3; 2:18; 6:23; Phil. 1:2; Col. 1:2; 2 Thess. 1:2; 1 Tim. 1:2; 2 Tim. 1:2; Titus 1:4; Philem. 1:3; James 1:17; 1 Pet. 1:3; 2 Pet. 1:17; 1 John 3:1; 4:14; 2 John 1:3.

18. Rom 15:6; 2 Cor. 1:3; Eph. 1:3; 2:18; 5:20; Phil. 2:11; 4:20; Col. 1:3, 12; 3:17; 1 Thess. 3:13; 1 Pet. 1:3; Rev. 1:6; see also Rom. 8:15; 1 Cor. 15:24; Gal. 4:6; Heb 12:9.

19. *Book of Common Prayer*, http://www.bcponline.org/DailyOffice/direct .html.

THREE

The Narrative's Arc

And I heard a loud voice from the throne saying, "Look! God's dwelling place is now among the people, and he will dwell with them. They will be his people, and God himself will be with them and be their God."

—*Revelation 21:3*

And, to crown all, there will be a deep, an intimate, an uninterrupted union with God; a constant communion with the Father and his Son Jesus Christ, through the Spirit; a continual enjoyment of the Three-One God, and of all the creatures in him!

—*John Wesley, "The New Creation," §18*

I have a vivid memory of the first cassette tapes I was ever given as a child. These two tapes did not belong to the collective pool of records and tapes I shared with my brother and sister. These were mine—Steve Green's *For God and God Alone* and Petra's *Not of This World.* They may have made a strange pairing, coming from such different genres, but I did not think anything of it. I listened to them over and over again. That level of exposure to those songs has locked them into my memory. Yet Green's songs of God's glory, enthronement over the universe, and creation's praise captured me more and made a stronger, more lasting impression. The album's title song, "God and God Alone," is one that affirms God's supremacy in all things. With lines like "From the mighty to the small, the glory in them all is God's and God's alone" and "God and God alone is fit to take the universe's throne," I was imprinted early on with a sense of awe over God's power and sovereignty.[1]

The Bible unfolds in a grand arc from its opening to closing chapters. An account of creation's beginning lies at the front cover, and creation's forever-after lies at the end. With all the ups and downs, forwards and backwards that fill the middle pages, the similarities and differences between the opening and closing chapters of the Bible communicate a great deal about the grand story in which all creation is located. If God will bring to completion what God began from the very beginning, it will be helpful to explore the way the Bible frames that story of fulfillment. In chapter 2 we explored some key characteristics of who God is and how that shapes the interactions between God and creation. Here we are looking at the unfolding narrative of the Creator-creation relationship, and some implications: *The presence of God is key across the whole arc.* We can see in the Bible's opening and closing texts the resounding affirmation that *creation has always been intended as God's dwelling place and at last will experience the full effects of God's unending presence.* Ultimately it is *God with us*—Immanuel—that makes all the difference in the world. Whether in the story's beginning, middle, or end, all glory, praise, joy, and desire is rightly for "God and God alone."

---

1. Not only was the style of music different between the Steve Green and Petra albums, but the message of the lyrics was also different. Petra's song "Not of This World" suggests a never-to-be-resolved conflict between believers and the world—as well as between God and the world—that culminates ultimately in believers departing from the world, with lines like "We are pilgrims in a strange land, we are so far from our homeland" and "This world will never want us here, we're not welcome in this world of wrong" and "But we must be of good cheer; he has overcome this world of darkness and soon we will depart from here."

Several implications of God's presence unfold in the narrative. The first blessing for creation that God's presence brings is *life*. At the beginning of creation's story it is dead. God moves the world from death to life. The earth is an uncultivated wilderness (Hebrew: *tohu*) and empty (Hebrew: *bohu*) in Genesis 1:2. The desolate earth is enshrouded in waters and darkness. The single variable that makes anything possible in that impossible situation is the presence and activity of God. As the Spirit of God blows and the Word beckons, a world is drawn forth in lively response to its Creator. The land and sea begin to swarm with life, and the living things themselves are blessed with reproductive capacities.

The presence of the Spirit and Word of God make the difference in the death-to-life movement of Genesis 1—from wasteland toward productivity, from passivity toward activity, from simplicity toward complexity, from singularity toward diversity, from emptiness toward fullness. As we saw in the last chapter, God blesses the world with life that has a particular character. An entire system of contributing members emerges. As God has engaged creation, every agent in the community functions for the sake of something beyond itself: indeed, for the well-being of the whole system. All things operate as their Creator does in pouring out love for the sake of others, instead of operating out of self-interest. As things come forth to reflect (glorify) the character of God, God calls things good. God blesses the living creatures, instructing them to "increase in number" and "fill" the world (vv. 22, 28). God's creation is meant to continue in its unfolding activities. At the conclusion of the sixth day, "God saw all that he had made, and it was very good" (v. 31). Everything is set toward a purpose and is very good, while at the same time the blessings and commands seem to imply that further multiplication, filling, and activity lies ahead for the world. Days 1–6 do not give the impression of all creative unfolding coming to a close. The work is not done, even while provisions have now been put in place for the community to flourish.

In Revelation 21–22, creation receives the fullness of life from God's indwelling: "Look! God's dwelling place is now among the people, and he will dwell with them. They will be his people, and God himself will be with them and be their God" (Rev. 21:3; Ezek. 37:27; 48:35). Everything is so alive in the glory of God's presence that nothing remains in the world that evokes crying or pain (Rev. 21:4). As creation's Beginning and End, God gives "the water of life" for the life of the world (v. 6; see also 22:17; Isa. 33:16, 21; John 4:10–14). This water of life flows into the world as a river from the very "throne of God and of the Lamb" (Rev. 22:1; Ezek. 47:1–12). On the banks of this river of life, the tree of life makes its appearance once again in God's creation (Rev. 22:2, 14, 19). The nations are healed, the curse is lifted, and night is no more (vv. 2–5; Ezek. 47:12). The reign of God in the world is fully come. Just as in Genesis 1:1–2:3 where there is no evening and morning on the seventh day of rest, there are no temporal boundaries in the age to come (Rev. 21:25). All creation will join in the ultimate Sabbath rest of the Creator, when all is right, just as it ought to be (Rom. 8:18–25; Heb. 4:1–13).

All this description in Revelation highlights a second feature of the Genesis 1 narrative that is key to God's intention for creation across Scripture. The earth is seen, from the beginning, as God's temple-dwelling place. There is a pattern to the days of Genesis 1 that points to a connection between God's creation and God's temple. In many creation narratives from the ancient cultures around Israel, there is a pattern that the world gets made, a temple is built for the creator-god, and the creator-god goes inside to rest. The

Genesis 1 account leaves out the middle feature from that pattern. There is no mention of a temple. God's creation of the world transitions directly into God resting. This feature of Genesis 1 likely communicated loudly to its earliest readers that the whole of the heavens and the earth that God created was itself the temple in which God rested.

Other features of the narrative add to this depiction of creation as God's temple. The order of the first three days of creation corresponds with the order of the second set of three days (days 1 and 4: light/lights; days 2 and 5: waters and air/fish and birds; days 3 and 6: land and plants/animals and humans).[2] The movement through the two sets of three days matches the movement of a person entering Solomon's temple (see 1 Kings 6–8).[3] The entry point to the temple itself was oriented eastward, to the first light of the day (Exod. 27:13; Num. 3:38), as well as the direction of the Lord's coming to fill the temple (Ezek. 43:1–5). The inner courtyard was open to the sky and had several water features. These water features included the massive bronze basin called "the Sea" (1 Kings 7:23) and ten additional basins of water (v. 38), five lining the outside of the north and south walls of the sanctuary building itself (v. 39). From the watery, open-air courtyard, a person entered the sanctuary building by passing between two massive pillars representative of the earth's own pillars (vv. 15–22; 2 Chron. 3:17).[4] The sanctuary building (land space) was covered in carv-

---

2. Readers of Genesis 1 sometimes wonder how there can be light (day 1) before there is a light source, such as the sun or stars (day 4). It is possible that the author of Genesis is more interested in preserving the literary structure than in conveying a sequence of scientific data. Thus, for literary and theological purposes, the text divides light and the lights into their own days. We miss the point of what the text is communicating if we get caught up in the question of science.

3. See William P. Brown, *The Seven Pillars of Creation: The Bible, Science, and the Ecology of Wonder* (New York: Oxford University Press, 2010), 40.

4. Walton, *The Lost World of Genesis One*, 81.

Israel's scriptures connect their sanctuary spaces with the entirety of creation as God's residence.

ings of plants—pomegranates and lilies outside (1 Kings 7:20, 22) and palm trees and flowers inside (6:29). Also inside the sanctuary was the table with the bread of the Presence on it (v. 48). Thus, as a person entered the temple from the east, the person passed through an open-air area with the various basins of water, and into a place ornamented with produce of the land. Then in the heart of the temple was the abiding presence of the Lord (or the seventh-day resting of the Lord).

The tabernacle of the Lord also was likened to creation through the way the origin of both the tabernacle and of creation is narrative. Just as the world's creation had a six-day structure, the instructions for the tabernacle were given in six units (see Exod. 25–31). Just as the creation of the world had a seventh day of rest, the instructions for the tabernacle had a seventh unit telling the people to observe the Sabbath (Exod. 31:12–17). Also, the completion of the tabernacle was marked by God's presence dwelling in the space (Exod. 40:34–38).

Israel's scriptures connect their sanctuary spaces with the entirety of creation as God's residence.[5] Even the lights of creation themselves have a worship function as they "serve as signs to mark sacred times, and days and years" (Gen. 1:14). The prophet Isaiah makes the connection concerning creation as God's temple dwelling: "This is what the LORD says: 'Heaven is my throne, and the earth is my footstool. Where is the house you will build for me? Where will my resting place be? Has not my hand made all these things, and so they came into being?' declares the LORD" (Isa. 66:1–2).

The connection of God in the world with the world being God's temple carries from the beginning through

---

5. See Vail, *Atonement and Salvation*, 26–27.

the end of the Old Testament, and it expands with Christ. In John's Gospel the theme of temple helps point readers to the new dynamic of creation's life that God is establishing. John draws upon Judaism's history with its temple to show the creation-wide implications for the Word coming in Christ. Just as creation (God's sanctuary) had been defiled by humanity's sin, the Jerusalem temple had also been defiled in 168–165 BCE.[6] The temple in Jerusalem was captured by Antiochus IV Epiphanes, and the altar was used for making sacrifices to a pagan god. In 165 BCE Judas Maccabaeus lead a Jewish revolt to win back the temple. It was then ritually purified of the defilement, a new altar was placed in the temple and dedicated for worship of God, and worship was reintroduced. Each year Israelites celebrated the Festival of Dedication (Hanukkah) to commemorate the reestablishment of right worship in the temple. In John 10:22 Jesus visited the temple at the Festival of Dedication. People were suspicious of him and wondered if he was there to re-defile the temple with blasphemy. Jesus's response did not focus on the microcosm of the Jerusalem temple. Instead, he focused on the macrocosm of creation. They were celebrating the purification of the temple, dedication of a new altar, and inauguration of temple worship. Yet Jesus was the one who was going to do that for creation at large, which had long been defiled. Jesus suggested that he himself is the new altar, dedicated by the Father and sent into the world (v. 36).[7]

---

6. For an explanation of the background of Hanukkah and Christ as the new altar, see Richard Bauckham, "The Holiness of Jesus and His Disciples in the Gospel of John," in *Holiness and Ecclesiology in the New Testament,* ed. by Kent E. Brower and Andy Johnson (Grand Rapids: William B. Eerdmans Publishing Company, 2007), 95–113.

7. Rick Williamson helpfully noted to me that John's Gospel has already identified Jesus as the temple prior to this scene in 1:51 and 2:19.

At Jesus's own sacrificial death, John brings other components of the world-temple into focus. On one hand are the components of a new altar and the reestablishment of right worship of God that have already been introduced in John 10. John depicts Jesus's crucifixion, resurrection, and ascension as his hour of glorification—him being lifted up. Rather than sweating blood in an agonizing prayer for the cup to pass, Jesus is ready to drink it (John 18:11). With all divine authority, he directs his own arrest (vv. 4–12). At his trial he is crowned (19:2), robed (v. 2), hailed (v. 3), seated in power (v. 13), and presented as King (v. 14). He also had no difficulty carrying his cross (v. 17), which itself would eventually bear a sign broadcasting him as King in the languages of the people, the government, and commerce (vv. 19–20). After such a long defilement of God's creation-sanctuary, God is rightly being exalted from the Altar. In, through, and with Christ's offering, all things can be joined into right alignment before the Lord.

Additionally, to fill out the picture of temple renewal, John appears to be playing off of Eden imagery from Genesis 2–3. Eden is a garden stylized similarly to Israel's sanctuaries. For example, Eden is oriented with its entrance to the east (Gen. 3:24). The rivers flowing from the garden and all the precious materials mentioned in the narrative have connections with features of sanctuary worship (compare Gen. 2:10–14; Exod. 28:15–21; 39:8–14; Ezek. 28:13–15; 47:1–11; and Rev. 21:18–21).[8] Through the images John includes, what is happening in and through Christ can be coupled with God's initial garden-sanctuary intentions for the world. As John says, "At the place where Jesus was crucified,

---

8. See Gordon J. Wenham, "Sanctuary Symbolism in the Garden of Eden Story," in Hess and Tsumura, eds., *I Studied Inscriptions from before the Flood: Ancient Near Eastern, Literary, and Linguistic Approaches to Genesis 1–11, Sources for Biblical and Theological Study*, vol. 4 (Winona Lake, IN: Eisenbrauns, 1994), 399–404.

there was a garden, and in the garden a new tomb, in which no one had ever been laid" (19:41).

Christ, the dedicated and newly inaugurated Altar, is in a garden, which has a never-before-defiled tomb. He is brought into the tomb, and the tomb soon starts looking like the holy of holies where the glory of God is enthroned over the ark of the covenant (see Heb. 6:19; 9:1–28; 10:5–25). When Mary Magdalene looked into the tomb, she saw "two angels in white, seated where Jesus's body had been, one at the head and the other at the foot" (John 20:12). The angels on the bench are like the cherubim on the lid of the ark, which is the mercy seat where the glory of God resides. Paul makes a similar suggestion by saying that Christ is put forward publicly as the "mercy seat" (*hilastērion* in the Greek), by which everyone can see the righteousness—or covenant faithfulness—of God displayed (Rom. 3:25).[9]

John's use of imagery implies God's creation-sanctuary itself being renewed, with worship being rightly established and the glory of God inhabiting creation. Jesus's hour— from his death, to resurrection, to ascension (that is, from the altar, to the holy of holies, to enthronement)—is God's glorification in God's sanctuary. It marks both restoration and the dawn of a new creation: "early on the first day of the week, while it was still dark" (John 20:1; Gen. 1:3–5). Jesus himself is gardening (John 20:15), just as the first humans were supposed to do in God's sanctuary (Gen. 2:15). Even the disciples are made alive in a manner like Adam to be participants with Christ in this rightly ordered life. "On the evening of that first day of the week . . . Jesus came and stood among them. . . . Jesus said, 'Peace be with you! As the Father has sent me, I am sending you.' And with that he breathed on them and said, 'Receive the Holy Spirit'" (John

---

9. See Vail, *Atonement and Salvation*, 86.

20:19, 21–22; see also 1 Cor. 15:45). While these things hearken back to the beginning, the manner of God's presence in the sanctuary and humanity's life in the glory of God move beyond the beginning; they are new.

All divine-creaturely communion that Israel's sanctuaries and practices were meant to mediate dissolve into Christ. Within the garden of God's creation, all creation is gathered into the fellowship of God, in Christ, by the very Spirit by whom we call out "Abba, Father" (Rom. 8:15; Gal. 4:6). Christ is the temple (John 2:19–21), high priest (Heb. 3:1), sacrifice (Heb. 7:27), altar (John 10:36), curtain to the holy of holies (Heb. 10:20), and mercy seat (Rom. 3:25).[10] It is not that the world needed a replacement temple so much so as that temple life (in human-made temples) now becomes unmediated fellowship with God through Christ by the Spirit (in God's creation-sanctuary). In making creation new, all facets of fellowship with God that were mediated through Israel's temple arrangements move into Christ. This Mediator is the I AM—the very One with whom we are meant to have fellowship. As Revelation 21:2–3 says, God, in God's unveiled glory, comes to inhabit creation (see also Gen. 2:1–3; Exod. 40:34–38; 1 Kings 8:10–12). There is no place to go to visit God and no avenue to God but through God's own self—the Word made flesh. God's presence is not contained within or mediated by anything that is not God's own self—"the Lord God Almighty and the Lamb are its temple" (Rev. 21:22). Focus shifts in Christ from the Jerusalem temple to a public display of all to which the temple pointed about God's place in creation. As the prophets promised, there will be direct guidance from the Lord every

10. See Andy Johnson, "The 'New Creation,' the Crucified and Risen Christ, and the Temple: A Pauline Audience for Mark," *Journal of Theological Interpretation* 1.2 (2007): 171–91.

moment: "Then the LORD will create over all of Mount Zion and over those who assemble there a cloud of smoke by day and a glow of flaming fire by night; over everything the glory will be a canopy" (Isa. 4:5; see also Exod. 13:21–22).[11]

God's presence in the world has special implications for certain features of creation. In the Genesis 1 narrative there are three respective realms (heaven, waters, and earth), each with its component parts.[12] The first realm, heaven, has light, the firmament, and luminaries. Out of the second realm, the waters, come the seas, land, water creatures, and birds. And finally the named land is the realm of the earth, which has vegetation, animals, and human beings. Out of all these components of creation, the light(s) and humankind share direct connection with God. God does not call to the waters, land, or any part of the world to act with light(s) and humans. Rather, what is spoken by God is fulfilled by God alone ("Let there be," Gen. 1:3, 14–18; "Let us make," vv. 26–27).[13] God is directly connected with these two features in creation. In turn, the lights and humans alone have governing roles in the text (vv. 16–18, 26–28).[14] Both are specially related to the Creator through "special acts of creation, while at the same time

---

11. Donald E. Gowan, *Eschatology in the Old Testament* (Philadelphia: Fortress Press, 1986), 12–13.

12. William P. Brown, *Structure, Role, and Ideology in the Hebrew and Greek Texts of Genesis 1:1–2:3* (Atlanta: Scholars Press, 1993), 36.

13. See Brown's analysis of light and humans in *Structure, Role, and Ideology*, 40. What are readers to think about light, of there being no reference to any intervening divine action? Is God's speech self-referential, thus connecting light directly to the way God elects to exist in and for this creation? Revelation 21:23 may retrospectively offer this interpretation to Genesis 1:3: "The city does not need the sun or the moon to shine on it, for the glory of God gives it light, and the Lamb is its lamp."

14. The Septuagint version of Genesis 1 uses the word *archē* (govern) for lights and humans alone. The Hebrew does not make the connection quite as strongly since it uses two different words.

retaining their associations with the 'heaven' and 'earth,' respectively."[15]

In Revelation 21–22—when we see heaven coming together with the earth, in the descent of the New Jerusalem (21:2) and the declaration that "God's dwelling place is now among the people" (v. 3)—we hear the implications for God's two distinctive creations from Genesis 1. On one hand, "The city does not need the sun or the moon to shine on it, for the glory of God gives it light, and the Lamb is its lamp. The nations will walk by its light, and the kings of the earth will bring their splendor into it" (Rev. 21:23–24). Light is no longer mediated through luminaries or located above in the realm of heaven. It is directly connected with God's glory inhabiting the earth. On the other hand, humankind—intended to image God in governing the world—will "walk by its light." From across the world, humankind—"the kings of the earth" (v. 24) and "the nations" (v. 26)—will converge around the One with whom they share a direct bond. The "splendor" (v. 24), "glory," and "honor" (v. 26) brought by humans may suggest an improved reflection of the Lord's unveiled glory. God is the one in whom we were created to "live and move and have our being" (Acts 17:28). All creaturely glory is truly from God and unto God. The humans walk by the light from God as they in turn bring everything back into it (Rev. 21:24).

It is noteworthy, when all of this takes place, that Revelation mentions that the tree of life is present in creation but says nothing about the tree of the knowledge of good and evil.[16] I am not convinced the tree of the knowledge of

---

15. Brown, *Structure, Role, and Ideology*, 42.

16. I thank Rick Williamson for raising this question about the tree of the knowledge of good and evil in Revelation 22.

good and evil is absent so much as united into the imagery of the tree of life. In Genesis 2 the intended arrangement was for the tree of life and the tree of the knowledge of good and evil to be planted together in the garden—where human discernment is put in service to following God's life-giving pathways. In Revelation, this may so completely come to fulfillment that God's people are of one piece with God's blessings for the sake of the world (see Gen. 12:1–3; Exod. 19:4–6; 1 Pet. 2:5, 9). The prayer we pray at the sacrament of Communion would thus be fulfilled: "Come upon these gifts and upon us. Make them be for us Christ's body and blood, that we who receive them may be united with Christ and be for all the body of Christ" (United Methodist Church); or "Make them by the power of your Spirit to be for us the body and blood of Christ, that we may be for the world the body of Christ, redeemed by his blood" (Church of the Nazarene). Christ the One Life-Giving Fruit is so united to, nourishing for, and at work amid the covenant people of God—represented by the number twelve in the tree's "twelve crops of fruit" (Rev. 22:2)—that the tree of the knowledge of good and evil is indistinguishable from the tree of life; they have merged into one.[17]

Human ingenuity, discernment, or wisdom do not stand apart from or have any other purpose than service within God's life-giving pathways. Just as any person who delights in the ways of the Lord "is like a tree planted by streams of water, which yields its fruit in season and whose leaf does not wither" (Ps. 1:3), God's people, in communion with Christ as the tree of life, are planted on the banks of "the river of the water of life . . . flowing from the throne of God and of the Lamb" (Rev. 22:1); and, as a result, they are "bearing twelve crops of fruit, yielding its fruit every

---

17. See Ezek. 36:24–28; Vail, *Atonement and Salvation*, 51–62.

month. And the leaves of the tree are for the healing of the nations" (v. 2).[18]

It has perplexed interpreters of Revelation 22:2 why there is one tree of life, yet it stands "on each side of the river" that flows from the throne. It seems like "tree" should be plural, or it would somehow have to have the river flowing right through it. However, if the tree is a symbol of God's covenant people having such a part with Christ (John 13:8) that they share in the very life-giving mission of God in Christ (John 17:20–23, 26), then this singular people could line both sides of the river. This would not be the first time God's covenant people were settled on two sides of a river. When the Israelites settled the promised land, the tribes of Reuben, Gad, and half of Manasseh settled on the east side of the Jordan River, while the other nine and a half tribes settled on the other side (see Josh. 1:4, 12–15). Also, in Ezekiel's vision of the restored temple and land, there is a river flowing east out of the temple (47:1), with seven tribes getting east-to-west strips of land to the north of the river (48:1–7) and five to the south (48:23–29). Sandwiched between the tribes, moving out from the center, will be the temple (48:8, 10), a square portion for "the city" (vv. 15–20), the land for the priests (vv. 9–14), and the land for the prince (vv. 21–22). In short, there is more than one instance in Scripture where God's people have settled along two sides of a river, just as the tree of life is on two sides of the river in Revelation. All of this participation of the people in God's life-giving gift for the world is by grace. God's servants will truly serve God and the Lamb (Rev. 22:3) as

---

18. See Vail, *Atonement and Salvation*, 67–69.

they see the face of God (v. 4), bear God's name (v. 4), and receive God's light (v. 5).[19]

In the history of Christianity the classic answer about what is creation's final destiny or aim has been *the glory of God*. We are meant to shine fully in God—as Paul says it: "that God may be all in all" (1 Cor. 15:28). This is not because God is power-hungry or egotistical. God is not self-interested but is working for our well-being. "God is love" (1 John 4:8, 15). And "this is how God showed his love among us: he sent his one and only Son into the world that we might live through him. This is love: not that we loved God, but that he loved us and sent his Son as an atoning sacrifice for our sins" (vv. 9–10). God is gifting to creation the possibility of enjoying the richness of life God has in God's self—in the Father, Son, and Holy Spirit (1 John 4:7, 11–19). "We know and rely on the love God has for us. God is love. Whoever lives in love lives in God, and God in them" (v. 16). Our final destiny is the glory of God; there is no higher benefit creation could have. God is life. The Word was made flesh that we might have abundant life (John 10:10). With all creation we say heartily, *Thanks be to God!* We also pray with enthusiasm, *Come, Lord Jesus! Finish the work of new creation!*

In summary, the destiny of creation is the fullness of God's presence. The glory of God shining *throughin* every facet of creaturely communion will mean everlasting, abun-

---

19. It is tragic that Revelation 22:1–5 was ever separated from the end of Revelation 21. The Genesis 1–2 themes of God's light and humankind that are introduced in Rev. 21:22–27 do not end until 22:5. Thus, Rev. 21:22–22:5 needs to be read as a single unit. Also, Rev. 22:3–5 could be read in support of interpreting the tree of life in vv. 1–2 as a reference to God's people. Verses 3–5 explain what the angel showed John in vv. 1–2. Indeed, the last statement in verse 5 about reigning may share in the tradition of Luke 22:28–30.

dant life for creation and its inhabitants.[20] This life will be marked by the loving nature of God; all things will express themselves in loving nurture of their neighbors as their very selves. Secondly, connected with this idea of God's presence is the biblical theme that creation has always been and will always be the Lord's sanctuary. There is no time of day, season of the year, or place in all creation that is not sacred, to be consecrated as holy unto the Lord. The wisdom, righteousness, and justice of God's reign will bring an end to all sorrows, suffering, and death. All time and space are meant to be alive in the glorification of God. This is creation's gift from God, our Alpha and Omega, our Beginning and our End. In Christ, God's salvation for the world from the dominion of sin and death has dawned. Newly and rightly ordered life from and unto the unmediated glory of God has been inaugurated. The age to come is not waiting its turn for the present age to end. The kingdom of God is at hand. All thanks and praise be to God!

---

20. I realize "throughin" is not a word, but I wish the English language had the preposition "throughin" because "the preposition 'through' by itself can carry too much the notion of God's passing intersection with creation, with little or no interaction—unless it is taken in the sense of 'by means of.' The preposition 'throughout' can carry too much the notion of God's extension in space versus having a dynamic relation. Using 'in' [by itself] can be confusing in that either creation would be a container for God or there could be misunderstanding that the Spirit of God is creation's subjectivity and/or gets expressed by creation, or the Word of God *in*carnates as the substance and/or form of creation. With the word 'throughin' there would be both the movement of intersection between God and creation—thus avoiding pantheism or panentheism—as well as the friction of inwardness that circumvents a clean duality in terms of creation's utter separation from God. There is no creation apart from the acting presence of God *throughin* it" (Vail, "Creation out of Nothing Remodeled," in *Theologies of Creation: Creatio ex Nihilo and Its New Rivals*, ed. by Thomas Jay Oord [New York: Routledge, 2015], 62).

FOUR

Making All Things New

May the glory of the LORD endure forever; may the LORD rejoice in his works.

—Psalm 104:31

*You care for the land and water it; you enrich it abundantly. . . .
The grasslands of the wilderness overflow; the hills are clothed with
gladness. The meadows are covered with flocks and the valleys are
mantled with grain; they shout for joy and sing.*

—Psalm 65:9a, 12–13

*Let the heavens rejoice, let the earth be glad; let the sea resound, and
all that is in it. Let the fields be jubilant, and everything in them; let
all the trees of the forest sing for joy. Let all creation rejoice before the
LORD, for he comes, he comes to judge the earth. He will judge the
world in righteousness and the peoples in his faithfulness.*

—Psalm 96:11–13

*For the creation waits in eager expectation for the children of God to
be revealed. For the creation was subjected to frustration, not by its
own choice, but by the will of the one who subjected it, in hope that the
creation itself will be liberated from its bondage to decay and brought
into the freedom and glory of the children of God.*

—Romans 8:19–21

*"If I knew that tomorrow was the end of the world, I would plant an
apple tree today."*

—Attributed to Martin Luther

The Unbroken Line

In the arc of Scripture—from Genesis to Revelation—as the story goes through ups and downs, something is always preserved from the beginning point. A remnant always remains. A thread of continuity carries forward from the beginning of creation to the present. God faithfully preserves each component of God's beloved creation in order to bring it to its fulfillment. God is going to complete what God has started. God's beloved creation will not be cast aside.

In the theological framework laid in the opening chapters of Genesis, when God breathed life into the world and invited it into responsive expression, the world answered. The waters and land supported their inhabitants. The plants, animals, and humans produced. This was all meant to unfold in the goodness of God. But into all this God-gifted responsiveness, humankind introduced the language of violence (Gen. 4, 6). The tragedy of human sin has led to the death-directed corruption of creation's communion. Humans were meant to image God as a blessing to the earth and to fellow creatures. However, by Genesis 6, humans look like bad news when they "began to increase in number *on the earth*" (v. 1; emphasis added). This did not go unnoticed; "The LORD saw how great the wickedness of the human race had become *on the earth*. . . . The LORD regretted that he had made human beings *on the earth*, and his heart was deeply troubled" (v. 5a, 6, emphasis added).

This passage shows that the whole of God's creation holds a place in God's heart; the damage humans were doing was deeply troubling to God. The well-being of the earth was the focus of concern. From the beginning God has been acting on behalf of the whole sanctuary of creation, not just humans. The psalmist sings of God's care for the entirety of God's creation: "The LORD is good to all; he has compassion on all he has made" (Ps. 145:9). But, as Genesis 6 continues, "Now the earth was corrupt in God's sight and was full of violence. God saw how corrupt the earth had become, for all the people on earth had corrupted their ways" (Gen. 6:11–12).[1] This was not the holy dwelling place God intended the world to be. Out of God's great love, God was not going to abandon creation to this death-dealing corruption. Just as in the end of time, God's zeal for the earth-sanctuary means the destruction of "those who destroy the earth" (Rev. 11:18).

In the flood, God decided to give the world a bath—to purify it. God confided to Noah, "I am going to put an end to all people, for the earth is filled with violence because of them. I am surely going to destroy both them and the earth" (Gen. 6:13). This is a far different theology than earlier flood narratives of other ancient people,[2] such as the ancient Mesopotamian writing *The Epic of Gilgamesh*.[3] A key contrast between the epic's theology and the Bible's is that the assembly of the gods in the epic wanted to destroy every person—in one version because humans bothered the gods with their noisiness—and there was great anger that Utnapishtim survived the flood. He escaped drowning be-

---

1. As a model, when God placed the Israelites in the promised land, God's covenant people were not to have any part in the violent corruption of God's sanctuary space, the earth. "You shall not pollute the land in which you live; for blood pollutes the land, and no expiation can be made for the land, for the blood that is shed in it, except by the blood of the one who shed it. You shall not defile the land in which you live, in which I also dwell; for I the LORD dwell among the Israelites" (Numbers 35:33–34, NRSV).

2. There is a helpful video available to give some ancient Near Eastern comparisons: "Noah's Ark and Floods in the Ancient Near East: Crash Course World Mythology #16," Crash Course (created by John Green and Hank Green), https://youtu.be/VA3j5_vKQfc.

3. Several websites give a helpful overview of issues related to *The Epic of Gilgamesh*, including *Ancient History Encyclopedia* (https://www.ancient.eu/gilgamesh/) and *Institute for Creation Research* (https://www.icr.org/article/414/).

cause of a ploy among the gods, not because the assembly was working to redeem humankind and the world.

Since Genesis 1–11 offers a different theology of God's relationship with the world than the surrounding literature of the ancient Near East, the flood functioned as a reset button. While destruction was promised, creation was not wholly eliminated. Preservation was just as key to God's work to repair as any destruction. For example, the light and time-keeping luminaries of Genesis 1 were not removed from creation. The dome in the sky was not removed—only opened up so that the waters above could fall back down below. The land was not removed, but it was once again submerged; the waters that once had parted so land could appear sprang back up over it (7:11, NRSV). In many respects, the earth went back to the beginning point of Genesis 1:2 (see also Ps. 104:5–6). At the same time, remnants were preserved during the undoing of creation processes. Not only were the various parts preserved on the macro level (lights, dome, waters, and land), but God also preserved remnants of humankind and every earth creature in the three-tiered ark.[4] The various components with which God began, and representatives of things called forth to fill the empty earth, are those with which God continued.

In the flood story, the world went through an undoing and redoing of creation processes. Once the waters again stood above the land (Gen. 7:19–20) and all air-breathing animals died (vv. 21–23), God repeated the steps of Genesis 1 that had been reversed. The preparatory (prevenient) wind/Spirit of God blew again over the earth (8:1; see also 1:2). Light had not been taken away, so day one of creation

---

4. See David W. Cotter's comparison of the three tiers of creation with the ark having three tiers in his commentary, *Genesis: Berit Olam, Studies in Hebrew Narrative & Poetry* (Collegeville, MN: Liturgical Press, 2003), 55–56.

did not need to be redone. Day two needed revisiting. The dome in the sky was closed so that the waters above could again be separate (8:2; see also 1:6–7). The waters below needed to recede again, like they did on day three, so land could appear (8:3–9; see also 1:9–10). Also on day three the vegetation came forth from the earth, as it did after the flood with the symbolism of the dove bringing an olive leaf back to Noah (8:10–11; see also 1:11–12). The lights of day four had not been affected, so next the populating of the sky with birds on day five is symbolized when Noah's dove does not come back to him (8:12; see also 1:20–22). Finally comes day six and the repopulating of the land with creatures, including humans (8:13–19; see also 1:24–28). There is also a repetition of the day-six blessings, with some modifications (9:1–7; see also 1:28–30).

The destruction of the earth and its inhabitants (6:13) took creation through a reversal of creative processes. Yet there were remnants of every component preserved from before to after—perhaps with the one exception of plants. God was faithful to each facet of creation while it went through a wholesale act of judgment that was simultaneously purging and purifying. The flood was for the sake of mending creation's integrity. If creation itself was going to be repaired, it could not be utterly eliminated in the act of judgment; remnants of every facet had to be preserved for it all to be set right. The covenant God made after the flood extended and solidified the commitment God showed to creation through the flood. "Never again will I curse the ground because of humans. . . . And never again will I destroy all living creatures, as I have done" (8:21; see also 9:9–16). The plants also have assurance for unending cycles of "seedtime and harvest" (8:22; see also Isa. 55:8–13), along with the earth having days and seasons (Gen. 8:22; see also Isa. 54:7–10).

It is utterly maddening to God to see humankind destroy itself and the world by rejecting the love, life, wisdom, righteousness, justice, and peace God offers for creation's own bountiful well-being.

In a second example, God showed commitment to preserving God's creations by preserving a remnant of Israel through its exile. When God's covenant people persisted in their sin, God's purging of the promised land and the Israelites was going to be extensive. It would go on "until the cities lie ruined and without inhabitant, until the houses are left deserted and the fields ruined and ravaged, until the LORD has sent everyone far away and the land is utterly forsaken. And though a tenth remains in the land, it will again be laid waste" (Isa. 6:11–13). Yet with all that purging, there would still be a stump left over (v. 13; see also 11:1–5), a "surviving remnant of his people" (11:11) to gather from among the nations (11:11–12; 37:31–32; 46:3–4; 48:9–10; 49:6; 65:8–9).

There is no doubt that this type of discipline is painful (Prov. 3:11–12; Heb. 12:4–11)! However, it is out of love that God disciplines, so that the world and its inhabitants can come into the fullness of life God has for it, and not dissolve in corruption and death. God does not settle for either subpar life for God's creation or altogether losing creation to death. It is utterly maddening to God to see humankind destroy itself and the world by rejecting the love, life, wisdom, righteousness, justice, and peace God offers for creation's own bountiful well-being. It grieves the loving heart of God to watch this beloved world self-implode. That never-ending love will not stop until the world is gathered into the full blessing of divine life.

Across the Scriptures, humankind acts as the troublemaker. God does not respond by annihilating the entire line. God certainly intervenes to cut off (Gen. 19) or redirect (Gen. 11) various trends that compromise God's good intentions for creation. This is done for non-covenant and covenant people alike. The New Testament talks about God's interventions among God's covenant people through the metaphors of discipline (Heb. 12:4–11) and husbandry, such as pruning vines (John 15:2) and cutting down trees (Matt. 3:10; Luke 3:9). Jesus teaches in Mark 9:43–48 that we too should have this same posture. Whatever causes us to sin should be cut off—for example, our own hand, eye, or foot. By doing so, we can proceed toward life instead of to the destruction of Gehenna.[5]

God does not abandon what God begins. Not only does the thread of continuity carry through in acts of judgment like the flood and Israel's exile, but it also is shown in other divine interventions. The incarnation is a key example. When the Son of God became incarnate, God was working in continuity with humanity's starting point. With the incarnation, God did not form a new human line out of the dust and breathe the Spirit into it. Those processes are how God initiated the line of humankind with Adam (Gen. 2:7). Instead, God came into the already existing line of humanity (Luke 3:23–38). Rather than making a new humanity, God made humanity new. As the Holy Spirit overshadowed Mary, the Spirit was breathed into Mary's womb instead of into dust (Luke 1:35). She bore the Son of God, incarnate as truly human—one of us. He is the second Adam, not because he is a new human line but because he marks a new beginning within the human line. True, full humanity is brought back within the human story. The creative Word rewrites the human story from within. God does not jettison God's beloved creation but works from the dawn of time toward its fulfillment in God's life-giving blessings (for example, John 1:4; 3:16; 10:10).

---

5. See Kim Papaioannou, "Motifs of Death and Hell in the Teaching of Jesus, Part 2: An Examination of Gehenna," *Melanesian Journal of Theology* 33.1–2 (2017): 15–16. Gehenna will be examined in chapter 6.

Becoming incarnate in creation increased the stakes in God's mission for the sake of the world. God had already made multiple everlasting covenants in the Old Testament. God made everlasting covenants with the earth and all its inhabitants after the flood, the family of Abraham and Sarah, and King David. God's covenant faithfulness was already at stake in preserving the world and bringing it to the fullness of God's intentions. With the incarnation, now God literally has skin in the game. The Son of God has taken on full humanity and is two natures—divine and human—"without division, without separation" (Council of Chalcedon, AD 451). The union is permanent. The Son of God, like us, is of the very substance of creation—an earthling of the earth.[6] Were God to annihilate the substance of creation, it would now be an act of divine *self*-annihilation. The Son of God has become a sixth-day land creature, tied in relation and vocation to the earth and its inhabitants (Gen. 1:26–29; 2:4–8, 15). We come from the earth, live on the earth, depend on the produce of the earth, and are meant to tend the earth. Christ is no exception to this. There is a tiny detail in John's Gospel about the morning of Christ's resurrection that may not be so innocent; he was mistaken as the gardener in the garden in which he was crucified, buried, and resurrected to new life (John 19:41; 20:15). Gardening is the function humanity was always meant to fill in creation (Gen. 2:5-8, 15).[7] The glory of God's own nature is shown forth as love poured out for the sake of the world.[8] In Christ, we see what that looks like in

---

6. His humanity is no different than ours. In Hebrew that would make him *adam* (human) of the *adamah* (ground). In Latin he would be *human* of the *humus* (ground).

7. See N. T. Wright, *Surprised by Hope: Rethinking Heaven, the Resurrection, and the Mission of the Church* (New York: HarperOne, 2008), 210.

8. Scripture affirms for us that greatness is measured in serving (Matt. 20:25–28; Mark 10:42–45).

human nature. The divine Son serves among us, as one of us, for the sake of the very creation God so loves and has sent the Son into in unending union.

Making All Things New

God will bring creation to the fullness of its intended life in the glory of God. The Old and New Testaments offer images of what it will mean for creation when Jesus the Messiah returns and creation is made new. The prophets give us some of the most classic images of the earth's transformation into abundant life. When humankind and God's covenant people sin, it is *discreative*. Our *discreative* actions bring about a type of barrenness, desolation, and emptiness that looks much like the desperate situation of the world apart from God's creative intervention (Gen. 1:2; 2:4–5). Just like with the flood, when people sin, the land deteriorates to conditions prior to God's life-giving activity (see, for example, Isa. 27:7–11; 32:9–15 and Jer. 4:23–28; 22:5–7). "Making a place a desert—whether it is Canaan or any other land—is a sign of judgment (see Isa. 14:17; 17:2, 9; Jer. 17:5–8; 50:10–13; Zeph. 2:4, 13; and Mal. 1:3). Indeed, the destruction of Babylon in Jeremiah 51:42–43 is described as a reversal of the creation processes depicted in Genesis 1:2–10. On the other hand, salvation in Isaiah 35:1–4 and Ezekiel 36:1–12 is painted as a progression from empty desert to fruitful land (see Isa. 40:3; 41:17–20; 42:5–17)."[9]

When we sin, we truly subject creation to futility (Rom. 8:20).[10] Salvation for the earth's inhabitants is cor-

---

9. Vail, *Atonement and Salvation*, 144, note 5; see 22–23.

10. The grammar of this passage in Romans 8 offers no direct claim of who subjects creation to futility. My reading of humanity as the responsible subject is based on the broader context of the book and Scripture as a whole.

related with bountiful salvation for the earth itself.[11] Fixing how humanity lives is accompanied by healing for the earth. With humankind's fulfillment as God's children comes creation's liberation "from its bondage to decay" (Rom. 8:21). Creation itself will be "brought into the freedom and glory of the children of God" (v. 21). Joel 3:18 offers vivid symbolic language to depict God's fully redeemed earth: "In that day the mountains will drip new wine, and the hills will flow with milk; all the ravines of Judah will run with water. A fountain will flow out of the LORD's house and will water the valley of acacias." Here is a second example of the fulfillment of God's intentions for the earth from Isaiah 35:1–2 and verse 7: "The desert and the parched land will be glad; the wilderness will rejoice and blossom. Like the crocus, it will burst into bloom; it will rejoice greatly and shout for joy. The glory of Lebanon will be given to it, the splendor of Carmel and Sharon; they will see the glory of the LORD, the splendor of our God. . . . The burning sand will become a pool, the thirsty ground bubbling springs. In the haunts where jackals once lay, grass and reeds and papyrus will grow."[12]

The empty desert wilderness of Genesis 1:2 or 2:4–6 will not be the final destiny of the world. God is zealous to make creation the sanctuary God intends it to be, for its own sake of having abundant life in the glory of the Lord. But first, the earth must be cleansed of those who do not repent of the destruction they do to the earth (Rev. 11:18). Humankind must repent of its violent ways; hearts and actions must be set right. By the Spirit, we must become

---

11. Howard Snyder and Joel Scandrett's book title is correct: *Salvation Means Creation Healed*.

12. See Ps. 65, 148; Ezek. 34:25–29; 36:34–35; 47–48; and Joel 2:21–23.

participants in the new, resurrected life of the second Adam (John 20:15, 22).

It is not just that the land is to be blessed when humankind is healed of its violent ways. The violence in the relationships among animals and between humans and animals will also be healed. Humans were originally created to care for the animals, not eat them (Gen. 1:28–30). Our work was meant to nurture the well-being of others, not to be for our own gain. Eating animals was a concession God made after the flood (Gen. 9:1–3). The flood did not change human hearts (6:5; 8:21). But this concession carried with it conflict between humans and animals. The animals would dread the people created to care for them (9:2). Humans would eat the creatures they were created to nurture (v. 3). And animals would shed human blood (vv. 5–6). Isaiah 11:6–9 promises that the fullness of God's presence will bring an end to this economy of alienation and death within the creation-sanctuary: "The wolf will live with the lamb, the leopard will lie down with the goat, the calf and the lion and the yearling together; and a little child will lead them. The cow will feed with the bear, their young will lie down together, and the lion will eat straw like the ox. The infant will play near the cobra's den, and the young child will put its hand into the viper's nest. They will neither harm nor destroy on all my holy mountain, for the earth will be filled with the knowledge of the LORD as the waters cover the sea."[13]

It is impossible to say how this would all work at the practical level. Humans can survive on a vegetarian diet. However, many species are purely carnivorous and do not

---

13. In addition to this passage, in Isaiah 65:25 the Lord says, "The wolf and the lamb will feed together, and the lion will eat straw like the ox, and dust will be the serpent's food. They will neither harm nor destroy on all my holy mountain."

have the proper teeth or digestive systems to break down plant material. No matter whether this is to be taken literally, as some artists have painted it, or as a signpost pointing to the holistic transformation of all creation in the coming age, it will nevertheless require a divine act of new creation to bring about that new order. The old order will have to come to an end. The creatures will have to be made new. However, for the creatures and the present order of life to have salvation, it will have to be them who are transformed and not entirely new lines that are created. As in the pattern of Scripture, the *new* is the righting, transforming, and fulfilling of the old in the glory of God's presence. While we cannot understand exactly how it all will work—because it could never be brought about in the world as the world currently exists—Isaiah gives us a glimpse of what it would mean for all creatures to come into the fullness of life that matches the self-giving, other-nurturing love of the Creator.

Humans were created to function in the world as the very image of God. They were to care for the land and the creatures. When they decided to do what was right in their own eyes and invented their own pathways of violence, it not only disrupted their relationship with God, the land, and the animals, but it also disrupted their relationship with each other. Violence against fellow human beings became their mode of operation instead of nurturing the well-being of their neighbors. This too will be rectified according to the vision of Isaiah 2:2–4 (see also Rev. 21:22–22:5):

> In the last days the mountain of the LORD's temple will be established as the highest of the mountains; it will be exalted above the hills, and all nations will stream to it. Many peoples will come and say, "Come, let us go up to the mountain of the LORD, to the temple of the God of Jacob. He will teach us his ways, so that we may walk in his paths." The law will go out from Zion,

the word of the LORD from Jerusalem. He will judge between the nations and will settle disputes for many peoples. They will beat their swords into plowshares and their spears into pruning hooks. Nation will not take up sword against nation, nor will they train for war anymore.

Humans will finally get over using their ingenuity to maximize the design, manufacture, and use of killing tools. They will stop doing the *discreative* work of Sin and Death (Rom. 6).[14] They will walk in the Lord's paths and light. The nations will be healed (Rev. 22:2). And, like the resurrected Christ, they will get back to gardening with plowshares and pruning hooks. Their sole vocation will be the loving nurture of their neighbors—the earth and all its inhabitants.

These images are what will become of the world. We do not live in a posture of despair but one of hopeful anticipation. These images point to the destiny of God's creation when Christ returns and does a mighty work of new creation to refashion all things. That new creation work is not merely adjusting cultures, economies, ailments, understandings, and other things, as if we just enjoy an eternal golden age within the present nature of the world. New creation puts a period at the end of the way things are—the old passes away. It makes the present creation into something distinctly new. As the passages quoted above show, this coming salvation is for humans, animals, and the whole of creation. Human hearts, society, and nature will

---

14. Sin and Death are capitalized here because of the way the apostle Paul uses them in Romans. As Katherine Grieb explains, "Paul tends to personify Sin and Death, thinking of them as active powers" (*The Story of Romans: A Narrative Defense of God's Righteousness* [Louisville, KY: Westminster John Knox Press], 65). They hold us captive as slaves until we are set free in baptism, being united with Christ in his death and resurrection (Rom. 6).

all be transformed.[15] The receptivity of humankind and the land to the outpouring of God's presence will yield abundant results.[16]

From the Old Testament to the New, there is great hope expressed about the day of Christ's return, whether it is called "'the latter days,' 'the day of the Lord,' 'in that day,' or just 'that day.'"[17] It means judgment against wickedness and, thus, deliverance from wickedness.[18] For "the lofty— the powerful, the rich, the arrogant, those who oppose the poor, and those who disrespect God's sovereignty"—that day will be terrifying (Zeph. 3:1–8).[19] For the righteous, that day will bring salvation (Zeph. 3:9–20; Isa. 35; 65:8–16). This salvation will mean "the end of sin (Jer. 33:8), of war (Mic. 4:3), of human infirmity (Isa. 35:5–6a), of hunger (Ezek. 36:30), of killing or harming any living thing (Isa. 11:9a)."[20] Judgment clears away the chaff so that only justice,

---

15. Gowan, *Eschatology in the Old Testament*, xvii, 2. We can see this hope for all creation across the writings of God's covenant people. "Jewish eschatological hope was not just for the resurrection of individuals. It was hope for the future of God's whole creation. It was hope for *new* creation (cf. 1 Enoch 72:1; 91:16; 2 Bar. 44:12; L.A.B. 3:10; 2 Pet. 3:13, all inspired by Isa. 65:17; 66:22). This did not mean the replacement of this creation by another, as we can see from parallel references to the *renewal* of the creation (Jub. 1:29; 2 Bar. 32:6; 4 Ezra 7:75; cf. 1 Enoch 45:5)" (Richard Bauckham, *The Theology of the Book of Revelation* [Cambridge: Cambridge University Press, 1993], 49).

16. See Gowan, *Eschatology in the Old Testament*, 10, for an extensive list of various effects mentioned by the prophets: humankind (forgiveness—Is. 33:24; 40:2; Ez. 20:40–44; 43:7–9; Zech. 13:1; recreation—Is. 30:20–21; 59:21; Jer. 32:39–40), human society (peace—Is. 2:2–4; Mic. 4:1–4; conversion—Is. 66:18–23; Jer. 3:17; Zech. 2:11; 8:20–23), and the earth (fertility— Is. 4:2; Joel 2:23; 3:17–18; new order— Is. 11:6–9; 35:1–10; 65:17–18, 25; Ez. 47:1–12; Zech. 14:4–8, 10).

17. Walter C. Kaiser, *Preaching and Teaching the Last Things: Old Testament Eschatology for the Life of the Church* (Grand Rapids: Baker Academic, 2011), xiv.

18. Kaiser, *Preaching and Teaching the Last Things*, xiv.

19. Frederick James Murphy, *Apocalypticism in the Bible and Its World: A Comprehensive Introduction* (Grand Rapids: Baker Academic, 2012), 40–41.

20. Gowan, *Eschatology in the Old Testament*, 2. Gowan continues: "One of the distinctive features of these hopes is their sense of the radical wrongness of

righteousness, and peace will be present under the reign of God (Isa. 2:2–5; Ezek. 38:8, 16; Mic. 4:1–4).[21] This clearing away is why there is such resounding joy at the coming of God's judgment in righteousness (Ps. 96:11–13). Finally the back and forth between death (barren wilderness) and life (fruitful community) will end. Death will be no more, and life will pour forth among all things.[22]

The Bible speaks of two ages (eras, eons). There is "this" age and "the age to come" (Matt. 12:32; Mark 10:30; Luke 18:30; 1 Cor. 2:6). We currently live in this present age, under the shadow of sin and death. Even in this age, there is, nevertheless, the good news that God's reign "has come near" (Matt. 4:17; 10:7; Mark 1:15). In this age we already taste "the word of God and the powers of the coming age" as we share "in the Holy Spirit" (Heb. 6:4–5; see also Rom. 8:11). Even so, we pray for the day of Christ's return, when this first age will end and the next age will be total. We long for the return of our Savior from heaven (Phil. 3:20). God will come to dwell with creation "in the New Jerusalem that comes down out of heaven and abolishes the distinction between heaven and earth."[23]

While God's reign *has come near*, at the return of Christ the Lord's Prayer will finally be answered, and the will of God will be done "on earth as it is in heaven" (Matt. 6:10). Indeed, "our present sufferings are not worth comparing with the glory that will be revealed in us," and "creation

---

the present world and the conviction that radical changes, to make things right, will indeed occur 'in that day,' that is, at some time known only to God. The OT vision of the future deals throughout with the world in which we now live. All was made by God, so nothing is bad in itself, but sin has by now left it hopelessly corrupted. These texts promise transformation as the radical victory over evil" (2).

21. Kaiser, *Preaching and Teaching the Last Things*, xiii–xiv.
22. Murphy, *Apocalypticism in the Bible and Its World*, 10.
23. Bauckham, *Theology of the Book of Revelation*, 46.

itself will be liberated from its bondage to decay" (Rom. 8:18, 21). Believers and creation await this day in solidarity. "We know that the whole creation has been groaning as in the pains of childbirth right up to the present time. Not only so, but we ourselves, who have the firstfruits of the Spirit, groan inwardly as we wait eagerly for our adoption to sonship, the redemption of our bodies. For in this hope we were saved" (Rom. 8:22–24). A key step in that day, toward the full salvation of our bodies and all created things, is the revelation of God's final judgment against wickedness (Rom. 2:5).[24] Sin and death will be no more. Their presence in God's good creation "obscures God's glory in the world."[25] With the elimination of all that ought not to be in God's creation, "this world will be indwelt by the splendor of God."[26]

Destruction's Function

At times in the Scriptures it may sound like the world is not going to have this salvation from decay, or participation in the life-giving glory of God in the age to come. At times it sounds like everything will be burned up in total destruction. However, the fires of God's judgment purge away what does not belong and leave what is holy. Numbers 16 contains a story that helps us see this. In this passage a man named Korah, along with 250 Israelite men, challenged the position of Moses and Aaron (vv. 1–3). A test was proposed to see if these challengers fell in line with God's wishes. The challengers were supposed to stand in front of the tabernacle holding copper censers with burning

---

24. Even so, judgment is currently "being revealed from heaven against all the godlessness and wickedness of people, who suppress the truth by their wickedness" (Rom. 1:18).

25. Bauckham, *Theology of the Book of Revelation*, 46–47.

26. Bauckham, *Theology of the Book of Revelation*, 47.

incense placed on them (vv. 4–7, 16–19). God's answer to their challenge was that "fire came out from the LORD and consumed the 250 men who were offering the incense" (v. 35). The deviant Israelites were purged from among the people. However, the copper censers made it through the fire, having been made holy by being offered—consecrated—to the Lord (v. 37). Since they were holy and passed through the fire, they were hammered into a covering for the altar (vv. 38–39).

Scripture uses many metaphors that follow this pattern of eliminating wickedness and leaving untouched what belongs. For example, God's works of judgment are like the fires used in refining metal (Ps. 66:10; Isa. 48:10; Jer. 9:7; Dan. 11:35; Zech. 13:9; Mal. 3:2–3). Paul uses this metaphor of refining, which brings out what is valuable and eliminates impurities: "If anyone builds on this foundation [Christ] using gold, silver, costly stones, wood, hay or straw, their work will be shown for what it is, because the Day will bring it to light. It will be revealed with fire, and the fire will test the quality of each person's work. If what has been built survives, the builder will receive a reward. If it is burned up, the builder will suffer loss but yet will be saved—even though only as one escaping through the flames" (1 Cor. 3:12–15).

Second Peter also has a passage about fire on "the day of judgment and destruction of the ungodly" (2 Pet. 3:7; see also Mal. 4:1–3).[27] God is being slow and patient in bringing about that judgment day because God wants everyone to repent (2 Pet. 3:9, 15). But those who remain ungodly will face destruction in the judgment fire on that eventual day.

---

27. Daniel 3 offers a story filled with irony that Nebuchadnezzar's fire of judgment killed his own people (v. 22) but left God's faithful servants untouched (vv. 25–27).

According to this imagery, "the elements will melt in the heat" (v. 12). Everything "will be dissolved with fire" (v. 10, NRSV). Through the dissolving "the earth and everything done in it will be laid bare" (v. 10). Heating up the elements in this smelting process discloses what each one is. The dross can then be removed—destroyed (v. 7). What comes out on the other side, when godlessness is eliminated, is "a new heaven and a new earth, where righteousness dwells" (v. 13). Already, before that day, believers should "make every effort to be found spotless, blameless and at peace with him" (v. 14).

The smelting accomplishes its intended purpose of purifying, but we do not want to suffer great loss, like the builder in Paul's analogy. There are other metaphors about fire that follow this pattern of taking away and leaving behind. The weeds and chaff burn away, leaving the wheat behind (Matt. 3:12; 13:30, 40; Luke 3:17). The unfruitful branches are burned, and the vine is left behind (John 15:6). Like in the flood, being taken away is never a good thing in the Bible; being left behind to live in the land is the good thing. Taken people are the ones who end up dead, circled by gathering vultures (Luke 17:37).

The change from this age to the coming age is drastic. It will mean the end of the world *as we know it.*[28] It does not mean the end of the world in the sense that it will cease to exist. That which is eliminated has refused to be set right and receive the salvation for which creation groans. There are many phrases that the Scriptures use to describe the end of the present age in the transition to the next age: the sun darkening and moon turning to blood (Joel 2:31), the stars dissolving or falling, and the heavens rolling up like

---

28. See Greg Boyd's sermon "The End of the World as You Know It," https://www.youtube.com/watch?v=HoWHzuYF798.

a scroll (Isa. 34:4; see also Matt. 24:29; Mark 13:25). There is no way to understand from a twenty-first-century perspective how any of these will transpire. A dark sun would put an end to earth's life processes. Stars cannot in any literal way fall to earth. And we do not have a dome over our heads that holds up waters or is the place of the sun, moon, or stars; it cannot be rolled up like a scroll. These are figures of speech that are signals for the end of this age and the dynamics as we know them, and the transition to the next age. It means more than a change of leadership in the world. It will mean a transformation of the whole of the cosmos, not just part of it or humanity alone. God's unmediated presence in the creation-sanctuary will make all things new (Rev. 21:1–8, 22–23). The Scriptures indicate that this means an end of the world as we know it today; but ending the world as we know it does not mean ending the world. That same world will receive its King and the life of the age to come. Indeed, joy to the world! Let heaven and nature sing! We should not lose sight of the coming salvation for the earth and its inhabitants that comes through the process of judgment and new creation.

Methodius helps clarify the way the church has interpreted the imagery of fire and destruction in the Scriptures down through the ages. He writes:

> But it is not satisfactory to say that the universe will be utterly destroyed, and sea and air and sky will be no longer. For the whole world will be deluged with fire from heaven, and burnt for the purpose of purification and renewal; it will not, however, come to complete ruin and corruption. . . . The creation, then, after being restored to a better and more seemly state, remains, rejoicing and exulting over the children of God at the resurrection. . . . In reality God did not establish the universe in vain, or to no purpose but destruction,

as those weak-minded men say, but to exist, and be inhabited, and continue. Wherefore the earth and the heaven must exist again after the conflagration and shaking of all things.[29]

The biblical language of "destruction" can create confusion. Methodius noted a rebuttal that people may raise: "How then is it, if the universe be not destroyed, that the Lord says that 'heaven and earth shall pass away' [Mt 24:35]; and the prophet, that 'the heaven shall perish as smoke, and the earth shall grow old as a garment' [Isa 51:6]?"[30] He answers:

because it is usual for the Scriptures to call the change of the world from its present condition to a better and more glorious one, *destruction*; as its earlier form is lost in the change of all things to a state of greater splendour; for there is no contradiction nor absurdity in the Holy Scriptures. For not "the world" but the "fashion of this world" passes away [1 Corinthians 7:31], it is said. . . . We may expect that the creation will *pass away*, as if it were to perish in the burning, in order that it may be renewed, not however that it will be *destroyed*, that we who are renewed may dwell in a renewed world without taste of sorrow.[31]

There is a long history of Christians celebrating the Bible's teaching about new life for creation that awaits on the other side of the purifying fires.

---

29. Methodius, *From the Discourse on the Resurrection*, Part I.VIII, in *Fathers of the Third Century*, Ante-Nicene Fathers, vol. 6 (Edinburgh: T&T Clark, 1885), 365–66, https://ccel.org/ccel/methodius/resurrection/anf06. Methodius of Olympus lived from AD 250–311.

30. Methodius, *From the Discourse on the Resurrection*, Part 1.IX.

31. Methodius, *From the Discourse on the Resurrection*, Part 1.IX; emphasis added.

Summary

God is zealous to bring God's original creation to the full measure of blessing as the dwelling place of God. God always keeps the threads of creation going—the earth and its inhabitants. God's love is tenacious and will not give up. In the end, the earth, the animals, and humankind (as individuals and in their economic, political, and social relations) will see the complete salvation God has for them at the return of our Lord.

Human beings who walk in the ways of the Lord and not in the paths of the wicked will enjoy long life in the land (Exod. 30:12; Deut. 4:40; 11:8–28; 32:46–57; Jer. 35:12–16). But those who live godlessly, according to the ways of destruction rather than blessing, will have no inheritance in the coming reign of God in creation. Indeed, the meek "will inherit the earth" (Matt. 5:5).

The present age will have to come to an end. Creation will have to be transformed. All that is now will have to be created anew. All corruptions of sin and death will have to be eliminated—even within God's children (1 Cor. 3:12–15). All things pass through the purifying fires that eliminate any impurities. What is left will be recreated in the overwhelming presence of God, to have an entirely new kind of life—the life of the age to come. We cannot make incremental progress until we one day find we have brought humankind and all creation into the wondrous life of the age to come. Even while the kingdom of God is presently at hand, we will not evolve, progress, or work our way toward its fullness being manifest in the course of history. That does not mean, however, that we wait passively. Christ has already gone ahead of us into that resurrection life of the next age that will have no end. Death has no hold on him.

At the same time, Christ is still present to us in this age by the Spirit.

By being united with Christ in his death and resurrection through baptism (Rom. 6:4), we responsively participate in the life of the coming age, in the wind of the same Spirit who raised Christ from the dead (John 3:5–8). "If the Spirit of him who raised Jesus from the dead is living in you, he who raised Christ from the dead will also give life to your mortal bodies because of his Spirit who lives in you" (Rom. 8:11). Our call is to continual faithfulness. Our commission and promise from our resurrected Lord is to "go and make disciples of all nations, baptizing them in the name of the Father and of the Son and of the Holy Spirit, and teaching them to obey everything I have commanded you. And surely I am with you always, to the very end of the age" (Matt. 28:19–20). As new creations (2 Cor. 5:17), as preliminary participants in the life of the age to come, our life and work is to bear faithful witness in service under our Lord, the King of kings and Lord of lords, whose kingdom will have no end.

Isaiah 65:17–25 offers fantastic imagery of the promised transformation of creation.

> "See, I will create
> new heavens and a new earth.
> The former things will not be remembered,
> nor will they come to mind.
> But be glad and rejoice forever
> in what I will create,
> for I will create Jerusalem to be a delight
> and its people a joy.
> I will rejoice over Jerusalem
> and take delight in my people;
> the sound of weeping and of crying
> will be heard in it no more.

"Never again will there be in it
　　an infant who lives but a few days,
　　or an old man who does not live out his years;
the one who dies at a hundred
　　will be thought a mere child;
the one who fails to reach a hundred
　　will be considered accursed.
They will build houses and dwell in them;
　　they will plant vineyards and eat their fruit.
No longer will they build houses and others live in
them,
　　or plant and others eat.
For as the days of a tree,
　　so will be the days of my people;
my chosen ones will long enjoy
　　the work of their hands.
They will not labor in vain,
　　nor will they bear children doomed to misfortune;
for they will be a people blessed by the Lord,
　　they and their descendants with them.
Before they call I will answer;
　　while they are still speaking I will hear.
The wolf and the lamb will feed together,
　　and the lion will eat straw like the ox,
　　and dust will be the serpent's food.
They will neither harm nor destroy
　　on all my holy mountain,"
says the Lord.

FIVE

The Resurrection of the Dead

But Christ has indeed been raised from the dead, the firstfruits of those who have fallen asleep. For since death came through a man, the resurrection of the dead comes also through a man. For as in Adam all die, so in Christ all will be made alive. But each in turn: Christ, the firstfruits; then, when he comes, those who belong to him.

—1 Corinthians 15:20–23

The priests and the captain of the temple guard and the Sadducees came up to Peter and John while they were speaking to the people. They were greatly disturbed because the apostles were teaching the people, proclaiming in Jesus the resurrection of the dead.

—Acts 4:1–2

We look for the resurrection of the dead and the life of the world to come.

—Nicene Creed

Resurrection

Resurrection from the dead is one of the great mysteries of the Christian faith. At the same time, it is crucial. As Paul taught, Christ's resurrection is the linchpin of the Christian faith: "if Christ has not been raised, our preaching is useless and so is your faith" (1 Cor. 15:14). If Christ was not resurrected, and if we will not be resurrected, there are several implications for our faith (vv. 13–16): We would still be in our sins (v. 17), and every person who died would be forever lost (v. 18). In other words, our hope in Christ would be "only for this life" (v. 19); once death overcame us it would be all over for us. Death would rip us from God's hands and be forever victorious. Resurrection means the overcoming of every power that stands over us—the whole tangled web of sin and death (vv. 17–18). Resurrection overturns their victories, and their shackles are thrown off. Even more, in this triumph over death and the grave, death will never again be able to threaten us. Thus, resurrection is the completion of salvation. It is the full deliverance, healing, and transformation of all bodily life.

There is one, and only one, example of someone experiencing the fullness of resurrection from the dead: "Christ has indeed been raised from the dead, the firstfruits of those who have fallen asleep" (1 Cor. 15:20). Christ is the "firstborn from the dead" (Rev. 1:5; see also Col. 1:18). In both the Old and New Testaments there are people who died and were brought back to life again because God revived them (see, for example, 1 Kings 17:17–23; Mark 5:35–43; John 11:1–44; Acts 20:7–12). While these events were good news for the individuals brought back to life and for their network of family and friends, none of them was the same as Christ's resurrection. He is the first and only person at this point to experience true resurrection. In all those other instances, the person came back to life under the exact same conditions in which they had died. They were made alive again within this present age. They were able to go back to living, but they were still under the shadow of sin and death. Thus, they all died again. Christ alone is alive and free of the threat of death: "since Christ was raised from the dead, he cannot die again; death no longer has mastery over him" (Rom. 6:9). He alone has experienced transformation into resurrection life—the life of the age to come. In that age "there will be no more death" (Rev. 21:4; see also Rev. 20:14; 1 Cor. 15:26, 54).

A classic scripture for understanding (and misunderstanding) resurrection is 1 Corinthians 15.[1] It teaches us the type of change we look forward to when Christ returns and we are resurrected and death is removed from creation. At Christ's return, "the end will come, when he hands over the kingdom to God the Father after he has destroyed all dominion, authority and power. For he must reign until he has put all his enemies under his feet. The last enemy to be destroyed is death" (1 Cor. 15:24–26).

In this present age, we live with mortality. The shadow of death is ever present. As Paul teaches, when we die and are buried, we are buried in dishonor and weakness—a natural body (vv. 43–44). We are perishable, mortal creatures (v. 53). Throughout the entirety of the Scriptures, we are spoken of as dust that is inbreathed with life from God (Gen. 2:7; 3:19; Job 34:14–15; Ps. 104:29–30). We came from dust, we are dust, and we will return to dust (Gen. 3:19). Remaining alive is a gift from God (Gen. 6:3)—a gift no human or creature should take away. We do not continue to exist in this life or the next on account of some innate quality we possess—neither body nor soul.[2] Our life

---

1. To help navigate this chapter see Andy Johnson's two articles "On Removing a Trump Card: Flesh and Blood and the Reign of God," *Bulletin for Biblical Research* 13.2 (2003): 175–192; and "Turning the World Upside Down in 1 Corinthians 15: Apocalyptic Epistemology, the Resurrected Body, and the New Creation," *The Evangelical Quarterly* 75.4 (2003): 291–309.

2. Irenaeus, *Against Heresies*, 2.29.1 (note: in this sequence of three numbers, the first number is the book number, the second is the chapter number, and the third is the section number). Irenaeus of Lyons (approximately AD 130–202) is an important early writer because he was only two generations away from the apostle John. Irenaeus was able to learn from John's student Polycarp. Irenaeus produced one of the most comprehensive presentations of the apostles' teachings from the second century, a five-book work called *Against Heresies*, available

in this age and in the age to come is dependent upon God's life-giving activity. Irenaeus, who was a grandchild in the faith of the apostle John, taught, "It is the Father of all who imparts continuance for ever and ever on those who are saved. For life does not arise from us, nor from our own nature; but it is bestowed according to the grace of God. And therefore he who shall preserve the life bestowed upon him, and give thanks to him who imparted it, shall receive also length of days for ever and ever."[3]

As creatures we never stop being dependent on God. Nevertheless, there is a difference between our present bodily life and our bodily life when Christ returns and eliminates death (1 Cor. 15:26, 54; Rev. 21:4). In 1 Corinthians 15, Paul uses a metaphor of seeds and plants to explain that *difference* of bodily existence, even while showing *continuity* between what dies and is resurrected. In the normal workings of the world, different kinds of plants grow from different kinds of seeds—or, "to each kind of seed [God] gives its own body" (v. 38). We do not sow the final product—we sow only seeds (v. 37). There is continuity between the seeds planted in the ground and the plants that sprout from the seeds—even if the plants have differences from the seeds. As Paul moves through his metaphor, he notes similar things with resurrection. There are different kinds of seeds: "All flesh is not the same: People have one kind of flesh, animals have another, birds another and fish another" (v. 39). We should not expect the variety of seeds to all produce the same kind of plant, nor one kind of seed to change into a different kind of plant at the resurrection. The type we are is the type we will be. Yet at the same time, we

---

in this volume of translations from 1885: https://www.ccel.org/ccel/schaff /anf01.html. *Against Heresies* is often studied by scholars to understand how the apostles had explained Scripture to the first Christians.

3. Irenaeus, *Against Heresies*, 2.34.3.

are not sowing the final product. The splendor of the plant (resurrected bodies) will surpass the seed that is sown (vv. 40–44).

Christians continued to teach this continuity of kinds through the centuries. In the age to come all creatures will remain whatever they were in this age, "for each one among created things must remain in its own proper place."[4] Methodius further clarified that humans, then, will "be composed of soul and body" at the resurrection as God originally made us to be.[5] "For Christ at his coming did not proclaim that the human nature should, when it is immortal, be remoulded or transformed into another nature."[6] In fact, Christ himself did not take on flesh for no reason. He took it up to save it and then to raise it up. "For he truly was made man, and died, and not in mere appearance, but that he might truly be shown to be the first begotten from the dead, changing the earthy into the heavenly, and the mortal into the immortal."[7] In Christ "all will be made alive" (1 Cor. 15:22). Every body that is planted will sprout forth at the resurrection, since Christ is only "the firstfruits of those who have fallen asleep" (1 Cor. 15:20). Paul says the difference, or change, in our resurrected bodies from that which is planted will be that they are raised imperishable (vv. 42, 53), in glory and power (v. 43), immortal (v. 53), and spiritual (v. 44). Paul says very little about what will become of the wicked at Christ's return and, thus, tends to explain only what his *Christian* audience should anticipate. In the next chapter we will explore what the New Testament says about the wicked.

---

4. Methodius, *From the Discourse on the Resurrection*, Part 1.X.
5. Methodius, *From the Discourse on the Resurrection*, Part 1.XI.
6. Methodius, *From the Discourse on the Resurrection*, Part 1.X.
7. Methodius, *From the Discourse on the Resurrection*, Part 1.XIII.

In going ahead of us, he has created an entirely new kind of resurrection life for God's finite, physical creation.

The transformation from perishable to imperishable, dishonor to glory, weakness to power, and mortal to immortal sounds straightforward. We certainly have no experience of living where there is no corruption from sin, bodily frailties, or threat of dying. We can be injured, get sick, grow old, and even die. Something will certainly have to be changed about our bodies from our present experience of their workings for us to be imperishable and immortal. Still, the terms give us a sense of the type of healed, cleansed, and everlasting bodies that will be resurrected from the grave. This is precisely the change Christ experienced between living in this age, suffering crucifixion and death, and being buried, but then being raised into victory, entirely free of death's power. What was planted was raised as the firstfruits of the new life to come.

Only Christ has been raised into that type of bodily existence of the next age. He may have been resurrected three days after his crucifixion, but he was not raised back into this age that is subject to sin and death; he was raised into the life of the next age (John 14:1–3).[8] Christ has gone ahead of us, while still making post-resurrection appearances and continuing to be present to us in this age by the Spirit of God (John 14:15–27). In going ahead of us, he has created an entirely new kind of resurrection life for God's finite, physical creation. He made a way for creation and creatures to enter—through the resurrection of the dead—into the glory of the everlasting age to come, where death is no more. New Creation life has been made possible for us in him—the Way, Truth, and Life (John 14:5–14). Through Christ, though we may be outwardly wasting away (2 Cor. 4:16), even now we participate in communion with God,

---

8. See Gail R. O'Day's commentary on John 14 in vol. 9 of *The New Interpreter's Bible* (Nashville: Abingdon Press, 1995).

with fellow creatures, and with the earth in a manner that is a foretaste of the age to come.

Whatever everlasting existence is like, it is still physical. The resurrected Christ could be touched, seen, and heard. He could go for walks, break bread before his disciples, and eat meals. The New Testament is clear about *bodily*—flesh and bones—resurrection. Luke's Gospel says:

> While they were still talking about this, Jesus himself stood among them and said to them, "Peace be with you."
>
> They were startled and frightened, thinking they saw a ghost. He said to them, "Why are you troubled, and why do doubts rise in your minds? Look at my hands and my feet. It is I myself! Touch me and see; a ghost does not have flesh and bones, as you see I have."
>
> When he had said this, he showed them his hands and feet. And while they still did not believe it because of joy and amazement, he asked them, "Do you have anything here to eat?" They gave him a piece of broiled fish, and he took it and ate it in their presence. (Luke 24:36–43; see also Matt. 28:8–10; John 20:19–29; Acts 1:1–11).[9]

It is critical to affirm that Christ, in flesh and blood, experienced resurrection. Up from the grave he arose. The tomb was empty. God did not abandon Christ to the grave and will not abandon us. Early in the history of Christianity, Justin Martyr reminds us of God's commitment to the

---

9. See Andy Johnson's articles on Christ's resurrection appearances in Luke and Acts: "Our God Reigns: The Body of the Risen Lord in Luke 24," *Word & World* 22.2 (2002): 133–43; "Ripples of the Resurrection in the Triune Life of God: Reading Luke 24 with Eschatological and Trinitarian Eyes," *Horizons in Biblical Theology* 24.2 (2002): 87–110; "Resurrection, Ascension and the Developing Portrait of the God of Israel in Acts," *Scottish Journal of Theology* 57.2 (2004): 146–62.

physicality of God's creations. "For does not the word say, 'Let us make man in our image, and after our likeness?' What kind of man? Manifestly he means fleshly man. For the word says, 'And God took dust of the earth, and made man.' It is evident, therefore, that man made in the image of God was of flesh. Is it not, then absurd to say, that the flesh made by God in his own image is contemptible, and worth nothing?"[10]

Christ's own bodily resurrection and God's enduring commitment to creation in this age and the age to come should temper, then, the way that we understand Paul's statement that our natural bodies will be resurrected as spiritual bodies (*sōma pneumatikon*; 1 Cor. 15:44).[11] Paul's contrasts between "natural body" and "spiritual body," and "of the earth" and "of heaven" (v. 47) create a great deal of confusion. The confusion is compounded when Paul adds that "flesh and blood cannot inherit the kingdom of God" (v. 50). These statements make it sound like our resurrected existence is not physical—that we are raised immaterial or to a heavenly material.[12] Yet, just as Christ's "flesh and

---

10. Justin Martyr, *On the Resurrection*, in *The Apostolic Fathers with Justin Martyr and Irenaeus, Ante-Nicene Fathers*, vol. 1 (Edinburgh: T&T Clark, 1885), https://www.ccel.org/ccel/schaff/anf01.html. Justin lived from AD 100–165. During his life, he wrote several defenses of Christianity because of all the misunderstandings among the Roman elite, and he died as a martyr.

11. The work of Andy Johnson on 1 Corinthians 15 is quite helpful. See "Firstfruits and Death's Defeat: Metaphor in Paul's Rhetorical Strategy in 1 Cor 15:20-28," *Word & World* 16.4 (1996): 456-464; "Turning the World Upside Down in 1 Corinthians 15: Apocalyptic Epistemology, the Resurrected Body and the New Creation," *Evangelical Quarterly* 75.4 (2003): 291-309.

12. Andy Johnson, "Imagining the New Creation: On the Hermeneutical Priority of Jesus's Resurrection in Transformed Flesh," *The Oxford Institute of Methodist Theological Studies* (2002): 4, note 10, https://oxford-institute.org/2002-eleventh-institute/working-groups/. This confusion is not new. Irenaeus (AD 130–202) spent a significant portion of his final book in *Against Heresies* correcting false readings of 1 Corinthians 15 and other issues about eschatology. He carefully explains what the early church understood about Paul's statements.

bones" were resurrected (Luke 24:39), so too will our flesh and bones be raised to life. As Paul is trying to help his audience imagine in 1 Corinthians 15:44–49, Christ was raised with a "spiritual body," which is "a body that has been acted upon, transformed, and totally permeated by the life-giving Spirit [*pneuma*], making it appropriate for the new creation."[13]

We will not be souls, spirits, ghosts, or any other non-bodily creatures. What we are now versus what we will be is not a contrast between physical and non-physical. Rather, throughout Paul's writings he contrasts people who live merely by the flesh (or carnally) with those who live by the Spirit (Gal. 5:16–26). Those contrasting ways of living can be thought of as living out of our own resourcefulness (the flesh) versus living in the Lord (the Spirit). The fruits of each way of living are polar opposites.[14] Paul tells believers in Rome which manner of living they currently are to have. "You, however, are not in the realm of the flesh but are in the realm of the Spirit, if indeed the Spirit of God lives in you" (Rom. 8:9; see also 1 Cor. 2:6–16). Spiritual people, for Paul, are those who "partake of the Spirit."[15]

Being *spiritual* has nothing to do with being disembodied. People who are natural, carnal, or mere flesh and blood, are people who do not live according to the Spirit of God, or bear no fruit of the Spirit. Carnal people need

---

13. Johnson, "The 'New Creation,'" 186.

14. "But as the engrafted wild olive does not certainly lose the substance of its wood, but changes the quality of its fruit, and receives another name, being now not a wild olive, but a fruit-bearing olive, and is called so; so also, when man is grafted in by faith and receives the Spirit of God, he certainly does not lose the substance of flesh, but changes the quality of the fruit [brought forth, i.e.,] of his works, and receives another name, showing that he has become changed for the better, being now not [mere] flesh and blood, but a spiritual man, and is called such" (Irenaeus, *Against Heresies*, 5.10.2).

15. Irenaeus, *Against Heresies*, 5.6.1.

the Spirit's work within their bodies, not their bodies taken away.[16] Just as believers live by the Spirit in this life, we will have even more abundant life by the Spirit at the resurrection (2 Cor. 2:22). Paul is clear: "if the Spirit of him who raised Jesus from the dead is living in you, he who raised Christ from the dead will also give life to your mortal bodies because of his Spirit who lives in you" (Rom. 8:11). Essentially, "what is mortal may be swallowed up by life" (2 Cor. 5:4). This is not a doing away with our flesh and bones (being "unclothed"), but our flesh and bones being "clothed" or "swallowed up" in God's own life-giving Spirit (2 Cor. 5:1–5).

This gift of God's Spirit breaking from heaven into our earthly existence marks our present participation in God's kingdom (Luke 11:2, 13, 20), even as we continue to pray "your kingdom come, your will be done, on earth as it is in heaven" (Matt. 6:10). The gospel turns the dualism of the Greco-Roman world on its head, which had held that the physical realm is dreadful, heavy stuff that weighs us down and we need to shed it.[17] Instead, in the gospel, the very elements of the world, like our flesh, "will be transformed and incorporated into the 'new creation' at its consummation."[18] Thus, in the present we look forward to Christ's return and to the resurrection of our bodies. "We eagerly await a Savior from [heaven], the Lord Jesus Christ, who, by the power that enables him to bring everything under his control, will transform our lowly bodies so that they will be like his glorious body" (Phil. 3:20–21).[19]

---

16. For early Christian teachings on the contrast between flesh and Spirit, see Irenaeus, *Against Heresies*, 5.9.1 and 5.9.3; and Augustine, *On Christian Doctrine*, 1.24.25, https://faculty.georgetown.edu/jod/augustine/ddc1.html.

17. Johnson, "Turning the World Upside Down in 1 Corinthians 15," 291.

18. Johnson, "Turning the World Upside Down in 1 Corinthians 15," 292.

19. "The flesh, therefore, when destitute of the Spirit of God, is dead, not having life, and cannot possess the kingdom of God: [it is as] irrational blood, like

The Nicene Creed summarizes a number of biblical teachings when it says, "We look for the resurrection of the dead and the life of the world to come." Jesus's own ministry pointed toward what this ultimate completion of salvation for our bodies and the world will entail.

First, he healed bodies. Whether people were leprous, sick, bleeding, wounded, lame, deaf, or blind, he healed them. These healings all point to the restoration of bodies that comes when God's glorious reign is embodied in creation. Healings are signs in our present age; in our conditions of weakness and mortality, healings show what the kingdom of God is like. They are pointers toward the goal, not the goal itself. For creatures who are still subject to death, healings are temporary—a sign pointing toward God "making all things new" in the glory of God. The full manifestation of God's reign will surpass the present healing of our bodies and bring resurrection life to them. At Christ's return, we will experience the transformation of our bodies that the Scriptures promise.

Second, Jesus cast out demons. Jesus's ministry demonstrated that every agent aligned with opposing powers

---

water poured out upon the ground. And therefore he says, 'As is the earthy, such are they that are earthy.' But where the Spirit of the Father is, there is a living man; [there is] the rational blood preserved by God for the avenging [of those that shed it]; [there is] the flesh possessed by the Spirit, forgetful indeed of what belongs to it, and adopting the quality of the Spirit, being made conformable to the Word of God. And on this account he (the apostle) declares, 'As we have borne the image of him who is of the earth, we shall also bear the image of him who is from heaven.' What, therefore, is the earthly? That which was fashioned. And what is the heavenly? The Spirit. As therefore he says, when we were destitute of the celestial Spirit, we walked in former times in the oldness of the flesh, not obeying God; so now let us, receiving the Spirit, walk in newness of life, obeying God. Inasmuch, therefore, as without the Spirit of God we cannot be saved, the apostle exhorts us through faith and chaste conversation to preserve the Spirit of God, lest, having become non-participators of the Divine Spirit, we lose the kingdom of heaven; and he exclaims, that flesh in itself, and blood, cannot possess the kingdom of God" (Irenaeus, *Against Heresies*, 5.9.3).

and kingdoms was ultimately subject to the rule of God. Jesus's acts of deliverance for possessed people are signs of the coming deliverance, when all creation is freed from its bondage to all contending powers and principalities. This future and final act of salvation is a creation-wide deliverance, comparable to Israel's deliverance from Egyptian slavery.[20] All creation will be purged of all captivating corruptions, and those who align themselves with them.

Third, Jesus raised the dead. These acts point from within our present circumstances toward the full measure of salvation to come at the resurrection, when we are changed and death will be no more. Jesus's acts of healing, deliverance, and giving life (within the world as we know it) all point toward what everlasting life will be like in the resurrection and the life of the world to come. They bear witness to the coming kingdom of God.

In our twenty-first-century context, confessing bodily resurrection raises a host of questions. For instance, the healings, exorcisms, and resurrections that happened in Christ's ministry point toward what eternal bodily life will be. But that does not mean we can explain it. For many people, nothing remains, or finally will remain, of the "seed" planted in the ground. Not even dry bones remain (Ezek. 37). Not only have their bodies broken down, but the molecules that once formed them might also have been absorbed into other organisms. So how will each person be reconstituted at the resurrection? All through life—through eating, breathing, or even tissue transplants—we are trading substance with each other and with the broader world around us. Just breathing when near another person involves trading molecules. In answer to these questions, our hope in the resurrection does not involve re-gathering and enlivening the precise set of

20. See "The New Exodus," in Vail, *Atonement and Salvation*, 63–76.

molecules we had in this life. We do not place our hope for the resurrection in what we can accomplish through cryogenics, embalming, sealed caskets, or any other preservation techniques. Instead we commend ourselves into the Father's hands and place our trust in the re-creative work God will perform at the resurrection.

Such questions multiply. At what stage of life will we be at the resurrection? Will all the martyrs bear their wounds at the resurrection as their crowning glory, or are the marks of martyrdom peculiar to Jesus alone? The resurrected Jesus ate with his disciples; he was not a ghost. Such accounts raise questions regarding normal biological processes. What will they be for our resurrected bodies? Will we possess our immune, respiratory, circulatory, digestive, and nervous systems? How could they possibly function if there will be no more death, crying, or pain? How would we be impervious to what we have known in this life as life-threatening injuries, illnesses, or aging? We have only the resurrected Jesus for a case study, and the accounts of the eyewitnesses who saw him (1 Cor. 15:3–8). That does not give us enough information to answer our contemporary questions. Importantly, we are told in the Scriptures that bodily resurrection is more than resuscitating our bodies. It means transformation and making our bodies new. We will be further clothed with heavenly bodies that swallow up our present mortal existence (2 Cor. 5:4). We will be raised in the Holy Spirit in power, glory, and imperishability, just as Jesus was.

Other questions about the social systems we inhabit also arise. How will the diversity of cultures, worldviews, and technologies be addressed? Across time, people have had very different ways of living on the same land. How would they all experience a correction and renewal of all the relations familiar to them, with so many strange people and practices around? How many people, animals, plants, and organisms would a renewed earth hold? What era in earth's geological and environmental development might be represented in the new creation? Will tectonic plates continue to shift but without killing earth's inhabitants? How can the new creation be eternal when we know that even stars die—including the eventual earth-consuming expansion of our own sun before its death? What will the new creation mean for the increasing speed of the universe's expansion and cooling?

The Scriptures offer us signs that point toward the fullness of salvation. They speak of this present order of creation in the language and perspectives of their day about an order of creation in the coming age that is unlike what we experience now. The Scriptures point forward in a certain direction, but what we see ahead is hazy (1 Cor. 13:12). The entirety of who we are as humans will be delivered out of death and the grave. However, we presently have no context that permits us to understand what eternal life in a world saturated in God's presence is like.

The reign of God brings everlasting, whole, and uncorrupted life to bodily life in the world. It is at hand now, even while we wait for all contrary powers to be removed from creation (Mark 1:15; John 5:24). Salvation will be completed when Christ comes again and the dead are raised. We will all be changed. God's kingdom will forever and fully come on earth. We will be saved from sickness, corruption, principalities and powers, and death. This means that the effects are not just for us as individuals. There are social effects also. People whom Jesus healed did not remain social outsiders or beggars. They were reunited as full participants in the social, religious, and economic workings of their families and communities. Possessed people were delivered not only from their demons but also from self-harm, exploitation, and isolation (Mark 5:3–5; Acts 16:16–19). They were no longer grieving their families (Matt. 17:14–15) or communities (Mark 5:3–4) but were restored within them. Their deliverance freed them to be part of the group with dignity. The families of raised people were pleased to have them back. Deaths create great chasms in our lives where fellowship is no longer shared, roles are no longer filled, and resources are gone. Healing, delivering, and raising set things right; the world is re-fashioned as it should be.

When Christ returns, our present dysfunctions, enslavements, injustices, and losses are transformed into resurrection life. The social implications for all that has happened across history are profound. God will bring life, light, righteousness, restoration, and justice into every broken circumstance that has ever transpired in the world. Christ's own resurrection points to the social transformation resurrection brings. The disciples' betrayals were met with words of peace by the resurrected Christ. His absence in their gathering was replaced by his presence. Their sorrow was replaced with joy, their despair with hope. The injustices that had worked against Christ were overturned; he was vindicated. His demise was changed to victory, his dehumanization to quintessential humanity. Resurrection recasts and recreates all that was defaced under sin and death. All things are made new—bodies *and* their contexts. Indeed, life in the whole cosmos is transformed.

Until the Resurrection

One question the Christian belief in resurrection raises is how to imagine the condition, until the resurrection, of those who have died. A common narrative that circulates among Christians is that, when people die, their soul separates from their body, they are judged, and they exist eternally in heaven or hell (without their dead body). There is no need in that narrative for Christ to return and set all things right—including the elimination of all contrary powers, the reversal of death's grip on the dead, the judgment of all people, and the making of all things new. This common narrative has no interim between death and the everlasting life toward which we look. But, if Christianity confesses the resurrection of the dead, with Christ as only the firstfruits of the resurrection, then the present state of those who are dead is not their final state. John's vision in Revelation 20:13 still needs to happen: "The sea gave up the dead that were in it, and death and Hades gave up the dead that were in them, and each person was judged according to what they had done."

The Scriptures have many ways of talking about those who are dead. In the Old Testament there are different kinds of statements. One, for example, mentions people going to their ancestors when they are buried (Gen. 15:15). This association makes sense, given that many families buried their loved ones in the same cave generation after generation. Even so, more common is the claim about returning to dust (Gen. 3:19; Eccl. 3:20; 12:7) or descending into the pit (or Sheol; Job 33:24–28; Ps. 30:3, 9; Prov. 1:12; Isa. 14:9–11, 15). There is not any hope for those who go into the pit (Sheol). "What is gained," asks the psalmist, "if I am silenced, if I go down to the pit? Will the dust praise you? Will it proclaim your faithfulness?" (Ps. 30:9). Or, Isaiah writes, "In your love you kept me from the pit of destruction; you have put all my sins behind your back. For the grave cannot praise you, death cannot sing your praise; those who go down to the pit cannot hope for your faithfulness. The living, the living—they praise you, as I am doing today" (38:17b–19a). Death was seen as a one-way movement, a person's annihilation. Only by having living descendants who carried on the memory of the deceased did they live on. Frederick Murphy concludes, "Through most of the Hebrew Bible, there is no belief in the afterlife as we usually think of it. Where the continued existence of humans after death does come up, it is a shadowy existence in an underworld place called Sheol or the Pit, cut off from living humans and from God. There is no idea of rewards and punishments after death."[21] That would make death a sad and terrifying end.

By the time of the New Testament there was an increasing sense that those who had died did not simply dissolve into dusty nothingness, or that the pit of death meant only silence and darkness for people. Rather, to God every person is alive—whether living or dead (Ps. 139:7–12; Luke 20:38; Rom. 14:8–9; 1 Pet. 4:6). Certainly the dead must be resurrected to take part in the age to come (Luke 20:35), but being dead does not mean a person is dead to God. Christ himself entered the pit of death and the grave. Jesus predicted this about himself: "For as Jonah was three days and three nights in the belly of a huge fish, so the Son of Man will be three days and three nights in the heart of the earth" (Matt. 12:40).

Paul also explains Jesus's descent: "What does 'he ascended' mean except that he also descended to the lower, earthly regions? He who descended is the very one who ascended higher than all the heavens, in order to fill the whole universe" (Eph. 4:9–10).[22] No part of creation or condition of humankind—dead or alive—is without the

---

21. Murphy, *Apocalypticism in the Bible and Its World*, 68. "The first clear canonical reference we have to belief in such an afterlife among Jews is in Dan. 12 in around 167 BCE" (68).

22. For helpful background on Jesus's descent, see Richard Bauckham, "Descent to the Underworld," *The Anchor Bible Dictionary: Vol. 2* (New York: Doubleday, 1992), 156.

presence of God in Christ Jesus.[23] First Peter even mentions the possibility that Christ preached "to those who are now dead" (4:6). To God we do not cease to exist in death. At the same time, we do not believe in or put our hope for eternal life in some part of us being naturally immortal, like a soul. We are mortals, created through the Son and held together in him (Col. 1:16–17). God "alone is immortal" (1 Tim. 6:16).[24] We do "not rely on ourselves but on God, who raises the dead" (2 Cor. 1:9).

Just as Christ was "made alive in the Spirit" out of the grave (i.e., resurrected bodily), we too place all our trust and hope in God, whose Spirit truly is "the Lord, the giver of life" (Nicene Creed). God alone creates us and preserves us. Jesus points to his trust in and dependence on God at his own death: "Father, into your hands I commit my spirit" (Luke 23:46). We too commit ourselves into the Father's hands (Acts 7:59). We have no other hope. Only the Father, through the Son, by the Spirit, can hold us up in everlasting life.

Until the resurrection, while dead Christians are certainly alive to God in some way, the New Testament often describes them as asleep (Acts 13:36; 1 Cor. 15:6, 18, 20; 1 Thess. 4:14–15; 5:10); they "sleep in death" (1 Thess. 4:13). This condition does not cut us off from our future participation in resurrection life in the age to come, nor from continuing to abide in God. Indeed, because "we believe that Jesus died and rose again . . . we believe that God will bring with Jesus those who have fallen asleep in him" (1 Thess. 4:14). Dying does not change a person's status of being "in Christ" (v. 16). The coming of God's reign has broken down

23. See Vail, "Sin and Death in Mark's Gospel," *Atonement and Salvation*, 31–40.

24. Norman R. Gulley, "Death, New Testament," *Anchor Bible Dictionary: Vol. 2*, 110.

all barriers between heaven, earth, and the grave; God is infilling all dimensions of creaturely existence.

The heaven-earth boundary was "torn apart" at Christ's baptism (*schizō*; Mark 1:10, NRSV), and the earth-grave boundary was "torn apart" at Christ's death (*schizō*; Mark 15:38; see also Matt. 27:51–52).[25] As a result, we belong to God in living *or* dying: "If we live, we live for the Lord; and if we die, we die for the Lord. So, whether we live or die, we belong to the Lord. For this very reason, Christ died and returned to life so that he might be the Lord of both the dead and the living" (Rom. 14:8–9). God is present, and we are present to God, whether we go to the heavens or the deepest depths (Ps. 139:8). Thus, we can be as convinced as Paul "that neither death nor life, neither angels nor demons, neither the present nor the future, nor any powers, neither height nor depth, nor anything else in all creation, will be able to separate us from the love of God that is in Christ Jesus our Lord" (Rom. 8:38–39). Even if we die, we will "be with Christ" (Phil. 1:23) or "at home with the Lord" (2 Cor. 5:8–9). We can have confidence in death's inability to separate us from the love of God in Christ Jesus and our being kept by and in the enlivening presence of God while in death. Since we will be in the presence of God in death, we have no reason to doubt Christ's promise that we will be in "paradise" (Luke 23:43).

The New Testament gives us great comfort in knowing that every one of our deceased brothers and sisters in Christ are not lost. They are in no way separated from God. We commit them into the care of God to preserve them unto that day of Christ's return. In God alone do any of us have life, whether in life or in death. Yet their current condition

---

25. For an explanation of this boundary removal, see Vail, "Sin and Death in Mark's Gospel," *Atonement and Salvation*, 31–40.

of being dead must be overturned. For God to have the final say, for the fullness of salvation to come, for the dead to participate in everlasting life (rather than everlasting death), the dead must be raised (Luke 20:35). "By his power God raised the Lord from the dead, and he will raise us also" (1 Cor. 6:14; see also 2 Cor. 4:14). Death will have to give up its spoils (Rev. 20:13). If those who have died are never resurrected, then death wins; every circumstance we have endured of injustice, enslavement, weakness, corruption, and illness gets the final word (see 1 Cor. 15:16–19; Rev. 6:9–10). But we know we do not grieve like those "who have no hope" (1 Thess. 4:13). We know Christ will return and place all things under his feet, including doing away with death itself (1 Cor. 15:20–28). We know Christ will come again, bringing salvation to all bodies and creation, and his reign will have no end.

This has been the teaching of the New Testament, the confession of the church, and the comfort of Christians across traditions—including those in the Wesleyan-Holiness tradition. For example, H. F. Schmelzenbach, a missionary to Eswatini (formerly Swaziland), showed his hope in the resurrection in a letter he wrote on May 26, 1926, three days after the passing of his twenty-month-old son, Charles Kent. He conveyed that, after the funeral service, "the remains of our little darling was [sic] laid to rest under the Peniel trees to await the resurrection morn."[26] We not only have hope that death will not have the final word when it strikes, but our belief in Christ's return and the resurrection of the dead also give us boldness in how we conduct ourselves now (2 Cor. 4:13–14; 2 Tim. 4:1–2; Rev. 12:10–11).

---

26. Quoted in *Holiness Today* (May/June 2017), 17.

No threats, trials, or present losses can overcome the power of God in Christ Jesus to bring about our ultimate salvation—the resurrection of our bodies—and the making new of all things. God and God's people do not tuck tail and let sin and death win out in God's good creation. God is a loving, good Creator who is faithful to God's beloved creation. What God began in the beginning will be carried on to completion at Christ's return.

SIX

The Life to Follow

He will come again in glory to judge the living and the dead, and his kingdom will have no end.

—*Nicene Creed*

The previous chapter about the resurrection of the dead is meant to be paired with this one. That is the place to start before thinking about the eternal destiny of the wicked and the righteous. The focus of this chapter is to examine the traditions within the Bible concerning what will become of the wicked and the righteous at the end of this age at the final judgment. There is a long history of speculation in Christianity about both hell and heaven. This chapter does not seek to treat claims that arose in Christianity after the New Testament era. Rather, we will examine the Bible itself since it is the norm for all belief and practice. As we do, we will see in the Bible differences of perspective about the destiny of the dead as new ideas emerged over time. The biggest change is from the original perspective in the Bible that death was the end. Later, an idea developed of rewards and punishments after death for what people do in this life. The biblical explanations of how rewards and punishments happen are where so much diversity shows up. The tension is not entirely resolved in the Bible. There are, nevertheless, themes that we can discern.

Concerning the Wicked

Scholars have examined the biblical books in the sequence they were written and charted differences of belief that unfolded over time.[1] Books set in different periods of biblical history show changing perspectives on the destiny of the dead. In particular, scholars have noted substantial changes in the two centuries before the Christian era and in the first century AD. In those centuries Judaism adapted to communicating in Greek, along with explaining itself in relation to the culture of the Greco-Roman world. By the time of Christianity, old traditions in Judaism stood alongside emerging traditions. The contrasting views on death and resurrection held by the Sadducees and Pharisees, for example, clearly illustrate the diversity of views within Judaism in the first century (see Acts 23:6–8).

Death: Sheol and Hades

We know that the oldest view about death in the Bible is that it was permanent. At death, people returned to dust, descended to Sheol (the pit, the grave, the earth; Num. 16:30–33). This was neither a punishment nor a reward but simply the end. Given the preferred practice of burying all deceased family members in the same cave or tomb (Gen. 49:29–32; see also 25:8; 35:29), a person could also think of death and burial as being "gathered to their people" (see 49:29, 33) or that a person "rested with his ancestors" (1 Kings 2:10). In the earliest writings, there was no consciousness in death; people just break down into dust. Even while

---

1. For example, see Murphy, *Apocalypticism in the Bible and Its World*. Murphy offers a helpful charting of the emerging changes in perspective represented in the Old Testament.

ideas about Sheol shifted over the centuries, this belief about the destination of the dead is represented in the New Testament era as well: "the most common Jewish view in NT times was that all the dead descend to Sheol (Hades)."[2]

We can note here that Hades is a Greek term for the underworld that had various ideas associated with it in Greek thought.[3] Largely, Jewish sources leading up to the New Testament did not adopt Greek notions about Hades and merely used the word to communicate about Sheol.[4] However, 1 Enoch—a Jewish writing from early in the second century BC—suggests that all people in Hades are conscious and that the wicked experience punishment. There was, thus, an evolving sense among Jews and Christians in the first century that people are conscious in the realm of the dead and that, for wicked people, the descent into Hades would have some element of punishment with it—even though the Hebrew understanding of Sheol did not originally include consciousness or punishment.[5] Thus, there were differing ideas in the first century AD that Hades was either the place where the dead were "held in detention awaiting punishment at the last judgment"[6] or that it might

---

2. Bauckham, "Descent to the Underworld," 156.

3. As Kim Papaioannou explains, "Hades (ᾅδης) is a Greek term that comes from the verb ὁράω [horaō], 'to see' (infinitive, ἰδεῖν [idein]). With the negating prefix α it literally means, 'the place that is not seen.'" Papaioannou, "Motifs of Death and Hell in the Teaching of Jesus: Part 1—An Examination of Hades," *Melanesia Journal of Theology* 32.2 (2016): 104.

4. Papaioannou, "Motifs of Death and Hell in the Teaching of Jesus: Part 1," 103. In the Septuagint—the translation of the Hebrew Bible into Greek—Hades is used more than one hundred times as a translation of Sheol, and sometimes also for Hebrew terms like "silence," "pit," and "death" (Papaioannou, 105).

5. Philip S. Johnston, "Gehenna," *New Interpreter's Dictionary of the Bible D–H*, Vol. 2 (Nashville: Abingdon Press, 2007), 531.

6. Bauckham, "Descent to the Underworld," 154.

include already some preliminary punishment for the wicked.[7]

With the new idea about Hades including preliminary punishment for the wicked, there began to be theories that dead righteous people were held in a different part of Hades, or somewhere else until the final judgment.[8] For example, before the New Testament era, 1 Enoch 22 says that down in the earth all the dead are collected and separated "until the day of their judgment and the appointed time of the great judgment" (v. 4). The wicked and righteous are separated "by a chasm, by water, and by light above it" (v. 10). The righteous have access to the "spring of water with light upon it," but "the sinners are set apart when they die and are buried in the earth."[9] In the lifetime of the wicked, judgment had not come upon them. So, in Hades, the wicked experience suffering and torment even before the day of judgment.

There are only ten times in the New Testament that the word "Hades" is used (Matt. 11:23; 16:18; Luke 10:15; 16:23;

---

7. Johnston, "Gehenna," 531. As Philip Samuel Browning Helsel notes, "The New Testament contains various images of a 'negative' afterlife. Depending on the author's perspective, the unregenerate dead decomposed in their graves, suffered for a time before returning to God, or were separated from the believing and punished." Helsel, "Hades, Hell, and Sheol: The Reception History of the King James Version in American Fundamentalism," in *Heaven, Hell, and the Afterlife: Eternity in Judaism, Christianity, and Islam*, Vol. 2: *End Time and Afterlife in Christianity*, ed. by J. Harold Ellens (Santa Barbara: Praeger, 2013), 107. Paul, for instance, "does not seem to countenance everlasting punishment" (107). For a nuanced overview of the different words and beliefs about death and eternal punishment in Bible, see Rodney K. Duke, "Eternal Torment or Destruction? Interpreting Final Judgment Texts," *Evangelical Quarterly* 88.3 (2016/17): 237–58.

8. As early as the prophet Ezekiel (around 598 to 596 BCE) it may be that there were believed to be divisions in Sheol according to whether a person was circumcised (see Ezek. 32:19–3; see also Helsel, "Hades, Hell, and Sheol," 106).

9. James H. Charlesworth, ed., "1 Enoch," in *The Old Testament Pseudepigrapha* (Peabody, MA: Hendrickson Publishers, 2010), 25; see also R. Alan Culpepper, "The Gospel of Luke," *The New Interpreter's Bible*, Vol. IX (Nashville: Abingdon Press, 1995), 317.

Acts 2:27, 31; Rev. 1:18; 6:8; 20:13, 14). What to make of the word in Luke 16:23 is fiercely debated, and it has some features in common with the 1 Enoch 22 passage. In Luke 16:19–31, Lazarus and the rich man are separated at death (vv. 22–23), before the day of judgment, by a great chasm (v. 26), and Lazarus's side has the water (v. 24). It is not clear if they are in two different parts of Hades (one part like paradise and the other tormenting, like 1 Enoch 22), or if this unique passage in Scripture depicts only the wicked man in Hades and Lazarus in a different place.[10] Jesus's parable does not specify whether the current locations of the two men are their eternal locations. It certainly would not be the eternal location for Lazarus. Later, in Luke 20:35, Jesus talks about those who are "considered worthy of taking part in the age to come and in the resurrection from the dead" (but Acts 24:15 suggests a general resurrection: "there will be a resurrection of both the righteous and the wicked").

With the similarities of geography mentioned for the realm of the dead between 1 Enoch 22 and Luke 16, along with Luke only explicitly mentioning resurrection for the righteous (14:11; 20:36), it is possible that Luke follows the thinking in 1 Enoch 22:14 about the wicked staying in Hades: "A receptacle of this sort has been formed for the souls of unrighteous men, and of sinners; of those who have completed crime, and associated with the impious, whom they resemble. Their souls shall not be annihilated in the day of judgment, neither shall they arise from this place." Only after the New Testament period is this idea of two separate holding places for dead people significantly developed. Luke 16 is the lone example of this tradition within

---

10. In *Surprised by Hope*, N. T. Wright says that in this time period, and in Luke's Gospel specifically, "Paradise is . . . the blissful garden where God's people rest prior to the resurrection" (41).

Scripture.[11] As we will see, other traditions are represented in the rest of the New Testament.

Note, nevertheless, that in the periods of the Old and New Testaments, there is at least consistency that Sheol (Hebrew) and Hades (Greek) are the place where dead people go. Given this, it makes sense that Revelation 6:8 says the rider of the pale horse "was named Death, and Hades was following close behind him." Hades is what follows death. Upon Jesus's death, he descended to the place dead people go: "the lower, earthly regions" (Eph. 4:9–10; see Matt. 12:40). He was raised from Hades (Acts 2:24–32; the NIV translates "Hades" as the "realm of the dead" in vv. 27 and 31). Christ now holds "the keys of death and Hades" (Rev 1:18). The sea, death, and Hades will have to give up all the dead at the resurrection (Rev. 20:13).[12] Once they are defeated and vacated, death and Hades will be thrown in the lake of fire (v. 14). As Paul says in 1 Corinthians, "The last enemy to be destroyed is death" (15:26). With the removal of death, Hades, and the sea (Rev. 21:1), we see that "in new creation God makes creation eternally secure from any threat of destructive evil."[13] Nothing that destroys life will remain. The victory over death and the grave comes

---

11. See J. Harold Ellens, "Afterlife and Underworld in the Bible," in *Heaven, Hell and the Afterlife: Eternity in Judaism, Christianity, and Islam*, Vol. 1: *End Time and Afterlife in Judaism*, ed. by J. Harold Ellens (Santa Barbara: Praeger, 2013), 4.

12. There are some parallel statements to this in other writings around the NT period. For example, "In 4 Ezra 7:32 the earth gives back those who sleep in it. In 2 Baruch 42:8 the dust is called to give back that which does not belong to it" (Papaioannou, "Motifs of Death and Hell in the Teaching of Jesus: Part 1,"108).

13. Bauckham, *Theology of the Book of Revelation*, 53. Bauckham comments directly before this: "Following the destruction of the devil, death and Hades—the last of the destroyers of the earth—the new creation is characterized by one feature that makes it really, eschatologically new: 'the sea was no more.' . . . So the judgment of the old creation and the inauguration of the new is not so much a second flood as the final removal of the threat of another flood."

through the life-giving resurrection power of God for God's creatures; the power of divine life robs death of its captives.

Paul says, for instance, "When the perishable has been clothed with the imperishable, and the mortal with immortality, then the saying that is written will come true: 'Death has been swallowed up in victory.' 'Where, O death, is your victory? Where, O death, is your sting?'" (1 Cor. 15:54–55). When God dwells among us, "there will be no more death or mourning or crying or pain, for the old order of things has passed away" (Rev. 21:4; see v. 3). It makes sense that not only will death be no more when God is present but that there will also be no place for Hades—the realm of the dead—in the new order of things. Having been emptied, never to receive anyone through death in the age to come, it is discarded into the lake of fire.[14] Once death and Hades are in the lake of fire, which is "the second death," the lake of fire becomes the place where all persons are thrown whose names are not in the book of life (Rev. 20:15; see also 14:9–11; Ezek. 39:1–20).[15]

---

14. Ryan L. Hansen lists seven things not in the New Jerusalem: sea, death, mourning, crying, pain, the cursed, and night. Hansen, *Silence and Praise: Rhetorical Cosmology and Political Theology in the Book of Revelation* (Minneapolis: Fortress Press, 2014), 162. We can also note that Revelation 21–22 pairs well with Ezekiel's vision of restoration in Ezek. 47–48. Comparing those two passages, the New Jerusalem is also missing sacrifices, the priesthood, and the temple.

15. The New Testament is not the only place where the end of Sheol/Hades is taught. A Jewish writing from around the time of the New Testament says, "Bring to an end therefore henceforth mortality. And reprove accordingly the angel of death, and let your glory appear, and let the might of your beauty be known, and let Sheol be sealed so that from this time forward it may not receive the dead, and let the treasuries of souls restore those which are enclosed in them" (2 Baruch 21:22–23). Another source from the same time period says in a similar vein, "But when the years of the world shall be fulfilled, then shall the light cease and the darkness be quenched: and I will quicken the dead and raise up from the earth them that sleep: and [Hades] shall pay his debt and destruction give back which was committed unto him, that I may render unto every man according to his works and according to the fruit of their imaginations, even until I judge between the soul and the flesh. And the world shall rest, and death

It is not specified what "second death" means, given that death and Hades are not taking people but are themselves in the second death. The lake of fire is what Ryan Hansen calls an "unclassifiable space," since it is "beyond the bounds of observable and livable space."[16] It should at least be noted that this lake of fire, the second death, appears at the conclusion of the first age. It is nowhere described in the new heaven and earth in Revelation 21–22. Right after the judgment scene of Revelation 20:11–15, John's vision pivots: "Then I saw 'a new heaven and a new earth,' for the first heaven and the first earth had passed away, and there was no longer any sea. There will be no more death or mourning or crying or pain, for the old order of things has passed away" (21:1, 4b). Lack of any mention of the lake of fire in the reordering of all things

shall be quenched, and [Hades] shall shut his mouth. And the earth shall not be without birth, neither barren for them that dwell therein: and none shall be polluted that hath been justified in me" (Pseudo-Philo 3:10; *The Biblical Antiquities of Philo*, trans. by M. R. James; see Papaioannou, "Motifs of Death and Hell in the Teaching of Jesus: Part 1," 109). Revelation shares this tradition that death and any location that holds the dead has no place or function in the new creation. Death and Hades go into "the second death" (Rev. 20:14).

16. Hansen, *Silence and Praise*, 38. Hansen suggests that there are two "unclassifiable spaces" in this passage in Revelation 20 that are "beyond the bounds of observable and livable space." One is the lake of fire (vv. 10, 15), and the other is the "no place" (v. 11) of heaven and earth as they fled before the throne of God (see Dan. 7:9–14). The unholy trinity—Satan, the empire, and its public relations mechanisms—are also in the lake of fire (Rev. 19:20; 20:10; see Dan. 7:11–12). Duane F. Watson suggests the first death is our physical death in this age. The second death "is the final destruction of all that belongs to the realm of evil" ("Death, Second," *The Anchor Bible Dictionary: Vol. 2* [New York: Doubleday, 1992], 111). Revelation 20:10 specifically says the devil, the beast, and the false prophet "will be tormented day and night for ever and ever." There were varying traditions by the time of the NT on whether final judgment for the wicked would mean annihilation (1 Enoch 90:8–14; 99:2, 11; 108:3), everlasting torment (1 Enoch 22:9–14 and Philo), or remaining in the grave (some Jewish Targums). The way Papaioannou reads the sequence of death and Hades going into the lake of fire, the second death, followed by the wicked going into the lake, is that "Hades comes to an end when the wicked die the second death. There is now nobody else to die so death becomes defunct" ("Motifs of Death and Hell in the Teaching of Jesus: Part 1," 113).

does not prove its nonexistence in the next age. Nevertheless, its *location*—or lack thereof—in Revelation is consistent with other Jewish writings from before and around the time of the New Testament. In those writings the *location* for the wicked is not given "a geographical context," or it is "set free from any geographical constraints."[17] It becomes not of the world. No place is ever described for it when the heavens and the earth are made new for the age to come. This may also parallel how extreme the imagery of being cast into darkness is in Matthew 8:12, at the very point when the entirety of creation in the age to come is saturated in the unending light of God's glory (Rev. 21:23, 25; see also John 8:12).

We can see in these texts that there is a shift in the Bible from Sheol/Hades being the permanent place of the dead to being an interim place for the dead during this age, until the resurrection. In some of the final writings of the Old Testament this shift toward a resurrected life after Sheol/Hades already begins to take place. An apocalyptic worldview starts to become the way in which Israel, and eventually the New Testament, frames its understanding of the world. During the crushing upheaval of Judah's exile, the cosmic imagination of an apocalyptic worldview helped provide a way of capturing their experience. It also gave them hope—when all their experiences seemed hopeless—that God was still enthroned, their afflictions would one

---

17. Jonathan Lusthaus, "A History of Hell: The Jewish Origins of the Idea of *Gehenna* in the Gospels of Matthew and Mark," *Australian Religion Studies Review* (now *Journal for the Academic Study of Religion*) 21.2 (2008): 179. Regarding possible background for the lake of fire, see Duke, "Eternal Torment or Destruction?" 243–50. In Jewish writings from the time, there were two traditions that used "second death." As Duke writes, "in one tradition, it is the fate of the wicked that are never resurrected to life in the World to Come. In the other tradition, fitting the NT understanding better, it is the fate of the wicked that are first raised and then judged. In both traditions, a plain-sense reading indicates that 'second death' means that life has ceased for all time. There is no indication of a continued life in conscious torment or not" (248).

day be reversed, their enemies would one day be punished for the devastations they inflicted, they would be rewarded for remaining faithful, and God would set the whole cosmos right. In short, surely God is capable, faithful, and just to resolve the atrocities of this age as God establishes the age to come. Some of these changes on the way toward an apocalyptic worldview start to emerge during and after Israel's exile, starting in Ezekiel, followed by Isaiah 56–66 and Zechariah 9–14.[18] A full apocalyptic worldview is finally represented in the book of Daniel, including a clear statement about the resurrection of the dead (12:2).[19]

One part of the apocalyptic worldview is the belief that there will be rewards and punishments as part of the ending of this age; various elements typically accompany this belief, including a conclusion to this order of the cosmos, resurrection, a last judgment, the restoration of God's people, and transformation of the cosmos.[20] The shift that takes place in biblical teaching moves from expectations for what will happen to bring about idyllic circumstances for God's people *in history* to what will happen to bring about a whole transformation of the cosmos *at the end of history.* "Both the prophets of Israel and the apocalyptic writers concerned themselves with eschatology. For Israel's prophets, the expected future remained this-worldly. For apocalypses, there is an element of postmortem rewards and punishments."[21] In apocalyptic imagination there will be "an end to the present order that is cosmic in scope. Radical change is always in sight. Sometimes this means the end

---

18. Murphy, *Apocalypticism in the Bible and Its World*, 45–64.

19. "The first clear canonical reference we have to belief in such an afterlife among Jews is in Dan. 12 around 167 BCE" (Murphy, *Apocalypticism in the Bible and Its World*, 68).

20. Murphy, *Apocalypticism in the Bible and Its World*, 3.

21. Murphy, *Apocalypticism in the Bible and Its World*, 9.

of the world, but more frequently it means its transformation."[22] The coming day of judgment and salvation spoken about by the prophets could be readily translated into the apocalyptic worldview—that is, from the inauguration of a historical golden age for Israel to the inauguration of a new cosmic age.[23] In the apocalyptic worldview, there are various points of tension at work in this age: between the righteous and the wicked, the present and the future, forces on God's side and forces against God, those operating in the truth and those under a cloud of lies, adherence and infidelity, and more.[24] These points of tension will all be resolved at the end of the world as we know it, when the ideal for the world will come, the wicked and all sin are gone, and God's faithful remain.[25]

With the apocalyptic worldview—which shapes the last books of the Old Testament and the entirety of the New Testament[26]—came the teachings about resurrection of the dead, final judgment, and reward or punishment for deeds done in this life. The Nicene Creed summarizes these biblical themes as Christ "will come again in glory to judge the living and the dead."[27] There are two traditions in the Bible here about

---

22. Murphy, *Apocalypticism in the Bible and Its World*, 9.

23. See Kaiser, *Preaching and Teaching the Last Things*, xii–xvi.

24. Murphy, *Apocalypticism in the Bible and Its World*, 9.

25. Murphy, *Apocalypticism in the Bible and Its World*, 10.

26. Paul's letters are one example where the framework of an apocalyptic worldview shapes everything. As Beverly Gaventa puts it, "Paul's apocalyptic theology has to do with the conviction that in the death and resurrection of Jesus Christ, God has invaded the world as it is, thereby revealing the world's utter distortion and foolishness, reclaiming the world, and inaugurating a battle that will doubtless culminate in the triumph of God over all God's enemies (including the captors Sin and Death). This means that the gospel is first, last, and always about God's powerful and gracious initiative." Quoted in Philip G. Ziegler, *Militant Grace: The Apocalyptic Turn and the Future of Christian Theology* (Grand Rapids: Baker Academic, 2018), xiv.

27. The Apostles' Creed concurs. The Athanasian Creed expands upon these themes: Christ "shall come to judge the living and the dead. At whose coming

the judgment of the dead. On one hand, all of the dead will have to rejoin the living so everyone can face judgment: "there will be a resurrection of both the righteous and the wicked" (Acts 24:15; see also Dan. 12:2; Rev. 20:12–13). On the other hand, there will be a "resurrection of the righteous" (Luke 14:14). At the final judgment only "those who are considered worthy of taking part in the age to come and in the resurrection from the dead" will be raised (Luke 20:35). There is no way to smooth over that the New Testament affirms both of these as options of whether wicked dead people will be raised to face the final judgment.[28]

Gehenna

In addition to Sheol/Hades, "Gehenna" is a second term that factors significantly into what will become of the wicked. Gehenna is a Greek transliteration of the name of a valley that runs along the south/southwest edge of Jerusalem—the Valley of Hinnom, or *Ge-Hinnom*.[29] There are twelve references to Gehenna in the New Testament, almost exclusively used by Jesus in the Synoptic Gospels (Matt. 5:22, 29, 30; 10:28; 18:9; 23:15, 33; Mark 9:43, 45, 47; Luke 12:5; James 3:6). There are thirteen references to the valley in the Old Testament (Josh. 15:8; 18:16; 2 Kings 23:10; 2 Chron. 28:3; 33:6; Neh. 11:30; Jer. 7:31, 32; 19:2, 6; 32:35).

all men shall rise again with their bodies; and shall give account of their own works. And they that have done good shall go into life everlasting and they that have done evil into everlasting fire."

28. The Nicene and Apostles' Creeds are given weight in governing what counts as an orthodox reading of Scripture. They mention the judgment of the living and the dead (without mention of whether they are righteous or wicked). The Athanasian Creed does not conflict with any of the Ecumenical Councils; it is a helpful summary of orthodoxy that is used in many churches on Trinity Sunday. At the same time, it gets more specific than The Nicene and Apostles' Creeds by explicitly siding with scriptures that suggest a general resurrection of the righteous and wicked in order for them to face final judgment.

29. Papaioannou, "Motifs of Death and Hell in the Teaching of Jesus: Part 2," 8. See also Lusthaus, "A History of Hell," 175.

Several of these are purely geographic references. Many of the Old Testament occurrences mention the idolatrous sacrificing of children by fire that took place in that valley. In turn, Jeremiah speaks about God's response to these unthinkable practices in the Valley of Hinnom by making it "the Valley of Slaughter" (7:32; 19:6). It is common to talk about Gehenna as a garbage dump outside Jerusalem, but there is a lack of written references or archaeological evidence for that after the time of Josiah (seventh century BC) or in Jesus's day.[30] This leads Kim Papaioannou to the conclusion that

> Gehenna was not a rubbish dump outside Jerusalem. Neither was it a common word to denote hell. Rather, its origin lies in the prophecies of the OT prophets who depicted the final judgment in terms of a final eschatological war in which God would destroy the wicked in a valley outside Jerusalem. While in most of the prophets this valley is not specifically identified, in Jeremiah it was connected with the valley of Hinnom, Ge-hinnom. This rather obscure association lay dormant for centuries. Jesus is the first to resurrect it and creates a direct association between the [place name] Ge-hinnom/Gehenna and the final judgment. In other words, he is encouraging his audience, if they want to know what will happen to the wicked, to see how Jeremiah describes it in his Ge-hinnom passages. From Jesus the usage found its way into the Gospels, into other Christian writings, and eventually into later Jewish and Christian literature.[31]

---

30. Papaioannou, "Motifs of Death and Hell in the Teaching of Jesus: Part 2," 9.

31. Papaioannou, "Motifs of Death and Hell in the Teaching of Jesus: Part 2," 32. In looking up *Gehenna* in a standard reference source like the *Theological Dictionary of the New Testament* (*TDNT*), it says that there is a second-century

It is only the New Testament where we come to have Gehenna named as the destination for the wicked at the end of this age.[32]

As Papaioannou suggests, the references to judgment from the Old Testament prophets give the background imagery behind many of the New Testament references to judgment. For instance, Jeremiah calls the people of Judah to live faithfully in their land (7:2–4). However, if they persist in worshiping various gods, there will be consequences. First, God says, "I will thrust [Judah] from my presence, just as I did all your fellow Israelites, the people of Ephraim" (7:15). The people of Judah will be rejected and abandoned (v. 29). Along with this, "My anger and my wrath will be poured out on this place—on man and beast, on the trees of the field and on the crops of your land—and it will burn and not be quenched" (7:20). Specifically for the sacrifices they are making in the Valley of Hinnom (Topheth), Jeremiah says it will be called:

BCE reference to *Gehenna* as the place of judgment in Enoch 90:26; 27:1ff; 54:1ff; 56:3f. However, those passages do not name the valley, accursed valley, chasm, or abyss where the wicked will be cast. For example, they will "be cast into the chasm of the abyss of the valley...And they shall begin to fight among themselves. And their right hand shall be strong against themselves. And a man shall not know his brother, Nor a son his father or his mother, Till there be no number of the corpse through their slaughter, And their punishment be not in vain. In those days Sheol shall open its jaws, And they shall be swallowed up therein, And their destruction shall be at an end; Sheol shall devour the sinners in the presence of the elect" (56:3, 7-8; see Numbers 16:25-33). It is only in the notes on these passages of Enoch in A. Dillmann's 1851 translation that Dillmann names this place *Gehenna* and connects the unnamed valley in Enoch with the Valley of Hinnom in the prophets. The name "Hinnom" appears nowhere in the 1851 translation itself. Nevertheless, the *TDNT* follows A. Dillmann's notes as evidence of a tradition about *Gehenna* that predates Jesus's statements in the Gospels. Other fantastic commentators then follow the *TDNT* about the history of the term *Gehenna* (see, e.g., Peter H. Davids, *The Epistle of James*, The New International Greek Testament Commentary [Grand Rapids, MI: Eerdmans, 1982], 143).

32. Johnston, "Gehenna," 531.

the Valley of Slaughter, for they will bury the dead in Topheth until there is no more room. Then the carcasses of this people will become food for the birds and the wild animals, and there will be no one to frighten them away. I will bring an end to the sounds of joy and gladness and to the voices of bride and bridegroom in the towns of Judah and the streets of Jerusalem, for the land will become desolate.
(Jeremiah 7:32–34; see also 19:11)

Leaving bodies unburied "was an unspeakable horror. Even a criminal's corpse was to be buried (Deut. 21:23)."[33] If a person was neither among the living nor given a place among the dead, they were no place and, thus, no more. They were not placed in their family's burial place and remembered. It is not that unburied dead people were believed to be in limbo, restlessly roaming the earth; rather, they had no existence in the order of things.[34] Thus, in these acts of judgment, the *places* that the wicked were desecrating (and *discreating*) with their idolatry would become the place of their own desecration and *discreation*. We might say they were expunged from any record, affecting both humankind and the land.[35]

In Jeremiah 19 (another reference to the Valley of Hinnom), the people will die by the sword: "I will make them fall by the sword before their enemies, at the hands of

33. J. A. Thompson, *The Book of Jeremiah*, The New International Commentary on the Old Testament (Grand Rapids: William B. Eerdmans Publishing Company, 1980), 294.

34. These insights are thanks to my colleague Mike VanZant, who specializes in Old Testament studies. See also Duke, "Eternal Torment or Destruction?" 247–49.

35. In this type of desolate place there would be no settled people, no agriculture or urban activities (Thompson, 295, note 14). It is an additional tragedy of judgment that the fertility of any valley would be overtaken with the bodies of the dead (Jer. 49:4; Ezek. 37:1–2).

those who want to kill them, and I will give their carcasses as food to the birds and the wild animals" (v. 7; see also 2:23; 31:40; Joel 3:12–16). In the case of Jeremiah's prophecy to Judah, it is the king of Babylon who will do this to them (20:4–6). As a point of contrast, the prophet Ezekiel did not have the valleys filled so much as the slain lying on whatever ground they had desecrated with their idolatry (6:3; 31:12; 32:5; 35:8; 36:4). However, in one place Ezekiel speaks of an unnamed valley being filled with the hordes of Gog, to be feasted on by birds and wild animals (39:1–19). In Judah's history the Kidron Valley, which runs along the eastern side of Jerusalem, was also used several times for burning up artifacts used in worshiping other gods (2 Kings 23:4–6, 12; 2 Chron. 15:16; 29:16).

The prophet Isaiah also uses the location Topheth (Valley of Hinnom) as a warning image for the Assyrians, who were one of Judah's oppressors. In Isaiah 30:27–33, we hear of God's coming "with burning anger and dense clouds of smoke . . . his tongue is a consuming fire" (v. 27). Along with "raging anger and consuming fire" will be "cloudburst, thunderstorm and hail" (v. 30). God will strike down Assyria (v. 31). Here is the promised end for the Assyrian king: "Topheth has long been prepared; it has been made ready for the king. Its fire pit has been made deep and wide, with an abundance of fire and wood; the breath of the LORD, like a stream of burning sulfur, sets it ablaze" (v. 33). As Isaiah moves forward in 31:8–9, the sword that kills Assyria is not a human sword but terror and panic that will come "at the sight of the battle standard" of the Lord, "whose fire is in Zion, whose furnace is in Jerusalem" (v. 9).[36]

---

36. In a different chapter, Isaiah adds more imagery of consuming fire, beyond what will befall Assyria. "You [Judah] conceive chaff, you give birth to straw; your breath is a fire that consumes you. The peoples will be burned to ashes; like cut thornbushes they will be set ablaze. . . . The sinners in Zion are terri-

There are common features in Isaiah and other prophets to these acts of judgment: being cast from God's presence, killing the wicked by the sword (Isa. 66:16), giving them no place among the dead via burial, being desecrated by wild animals or open-air decomposition (v. 24), consuming the corpses with fire (v. 24), and returning the land to wilderness (Jer. 44:22; Isa. 34:11; see the Good News Translation). There are similarities in the judgment imagery, whether it is judgment of Israel (Isa. 29:1–16; 30:1–17; 31:1–7; 32:9–14; 33:1–19; 43:28), the nations (Isa. 30:27–29; 34:1–4), Assyria (Isa. 30:30–33; 31:8–9), or Edom (Isa. 34:5–15).

The prophets, nevertheless, are writing across the time period when God's people are transitioning in their theological worldview. They are transitioning from these historical acts of judgment against nations that afterward will bring about new historical circumstances. They are moving toward the later apocalyptic worldview, where there is a final judgment at the end of history, before the next age. Thus, in the prophets, these acts of judgment are followed in each instance with promises of the indwelling of the Lord, the Lord establishing justice and righteousness among the people, and/or the creative revitalization of the land (Isa. 29:17–24; 30:18–26; 32:1–5, 15–20; 33:20–24; 34:16–

---

fied; trembling grips the godless: 'Who of us can dwell with the consuming fire? Who of us can dwell with everlasting burning?'" (33:11–12, 14; see also 47:14; 66:15–16). In another prophecy of judgment against Edom—where there will be the end of the world as they know it (34:4)—the wicked will be given "over to slaughter. Their slain will be thrown out, their dead bodies will stink" (vv. 2–3). When the slaughter is completed (vv. 5–7), "Edom's streams will be turned into pitch, her dust into burning sulfur; her land will become blazing pitch! It will not be quenched night or day; its smoke will rise forever" (vv. 9–10). Partnered with this, their buildings will come down (v. 13), and their land will be changed back to uncultivated wilderness (34:10–11), where wild animals will flourish (vv. 11–17). So, Edom's "nobles will have nothing there to be called a kingdom, all her princes will vanish away" (v. 12).

There is no escaping that God alone is the Lord and Giver of life, on whom we must depend.

35:10; 44:1–5). This, then, qualifies the prophets' language about judgment. They say God's work of judgment cannot be avoided, stopped, or quenched: "No one can deliver out of my hand" (Isa. 43:13; see also Jer. 48:44–47). The sword will do its work, the wild animals will not be chased away, the worms will not stop eating, and the fire cannot be put out, nor will it fizzle out. In short, the prophets drive home that there is no disaster planning we can do to increase our chances of survival if we take part in wickedness.

Furthermore, "When I act, who can reverse it?" (Isa. 43:13). The Egyptians, for example, discovered at the Red Sea that they were powerless to oppose God or reverse God's judgment, which is both incontestable and final: "they lay there, never to rise again, extinguished, snuffed out like a wick" (Isa. 43:17). In the prophets, these acts of judgment against God's people and other nations illustrate the deadly result of living outside God's provision for life. Yet also in the prophets, when the people and land are purged of wickedness, there is the re-creation of the remaining people and land that follows. There is no escaping that God alone is the Lord and Giver of life, on whom we must depend. It is clear that the wicked cannot escape death or the desecration of their corpses, and humankind has no power of life in itself to reverse God's judgment. If God destroys, the only one who can reverse it and restore is God (Jer. 48:47; 49:39). In the pattern of the prophets, God does restore after the purging of the wicked is complete.

In the transition of the prophets' viewpoint toward an apocalyptic worldview, God's act of judgment is not *in history*, to be followed by a renewal *in history* of the people and land. Rather, the judgment of God comes at the *end of history*—the end of this age and the start of the age to come. That judgment in the apocalyptic viewpoint is just as inescapable as the prophets taught. But the stakes are not just whether people will be among the righteous remnant who enjoy the restoration in history, until the time of their own death. Rather, the stakes are everlasting.

Jesus brings forward the prophetic imagery of judgment into the cosmic, everlasting apocalyptic framework by using Jeremiah's Valley of Hinnom (Ge-Hinnom/Gehenna). There are times Jesus gives no accompanying details about what Gehenna will be like, other than being the place into which the bodies of the dead are thrown at final judgment (Matt. 5:29, 30; 23:33; Luke 12:5; Mark 9:45): "Fear him who, after your body has been killed, has authority to throw you into [Gehenna]" (Luke 12:5). It is possible he was counting on his audiences' familiarity with Jeremiah 7 and 19 and Isaiah 30, so he did not need to say any more about the facets of judgment that come upon the wicked. In Jesus's references, as in the prophets, dead bodies are thrown in Gehenna. While this would mean the dead would not be laid to rest in the earth (Sheol/Hades), there is no embellishment in the prophets or Jesus's use of Gehenna about whether this is conscious torment—not in the way one tradition about Hades had started to develop by the New Testament era (e.g., Luke 16). These are the bodies of already-dead people being thrown in Gehenna.

Interestingly, in Matthew 10:28 Jesus raises the stakes on the prophetic idea of the wicked being slain and their bodies being put into Gehenna. He takes away any possibility of enduring either outside the grave or in the realm of the dead (Sheol/Hades); in other words, he eliminates any hope in a process that can "kill the body but cannot kill the soul." There is a finality and totality to the judgment that is coming at the end of the age: "be afraid of the One who can destroy both soul and body in [Gehenna]" (Matt. 10:28). This destruction encompasses the totality of all we are, and there is no next step in the sequence, no fragmentation of existence or Sheol/Hades holding us for a future judgment beyond. There is no next *anything*. There is no coming back from Gehenna. (Perhaps this reality illuminates the nature of the "second death" connected with the lake of fire in Revelation.)

Other times Jesus adds in a few details from the prophets when he mentions Gehenna. He connects fire with Gehenna in Matthew 5:22; 18:9; and Mark 9:43 (see Isa. 30:30–33)—or worms and fire in Mark 9:48 (see Isa. 66:24). In a final place Jesus speaks about the teachers of the law and Pharisees being "a child of Gehenna" (Matt. 23:15), which is their destiny (v. 33), in contrast to the destiny of God's children being a destiny of blessing (Matt. 5:3–12).[37] The use of Gehenna in James 3:6 appears to follow the tradition of the prophets, as Jesus's statements in the Gospels do.[38]

---

37. Regarding adoption as children of God, see Vail, *Atonement and Salvation*, 108–11.

38. James 3:6 is the only reference to Gehenna in the New Testament outside of Jesus's statements in the Synoptic Gospels. This verse makes an interesting point of comparison to two prophetic statements: first, Jeremiah 5:14, "Therefore this is what the LORD God Almighty says: 'Because the people have spoken these words, I will make my words in your [Jeremiah's] mouth a fire and these people the wood it consumes'"; second, Isaiah 33:11, "You [Judah] conceive chaff, you give birth to straw; your breath is a fire that consumes you. The peoples will be burned to ashes." As in these two verses, James is also concerned with what our tongues are speaking; "The tongue also is a fire, a world of evil among the parts of the body. It corrupts the whole body, sets the whole course of one's life on fire" (3:6a; see Isa. 33:11). James's final statement in the verse is the difficult part. The tongue sets the person's life on fire, and then James says it "is itself set on fire by [Gehenna]" (3:6).

Many commentators suggest Gehenna is the source or birthplace of evil; thus, it sets our tongue on fire, and our tongue sets us on fire. However, the sequence of the verse ends with the fire of Gehenna rather than beginning with it. Also, the prophets do not typically associate fire with evil. Fire is associated with judgment: either the consequences of our own speech that burn us up (Isa. 33:11), or the wrath of God that will purge the earth of wickedness (Jer. 5:14). In the one Old Testament instance where Gehenna/Topheth is a place of judgment and fire is involved, the Lord's arm is "coming down with raging anger

Summary

Just as biblical studies on Sheol and Hades do not quite make them the full-blown notion of hell that we may have come to expect today, focused studies on Gehenna also do not take us to the robust features associated with hell that were developed in the centuries after the New Testament era. "The NT does not have the term hell anywhere in its text and does not moralize the eternal abode of the righteous and unrighteous."[39] With the whole range of ideas surrounding death, judgment of the wicked, and punishment, there is a history of development in the ideas and different traditions represented in the Scriptures—even within the New Testament itself. With the focused studies on the eleven New Testament occurrences of Hades and the thirteen New Testament occurrences of Gehenna, we can see that they function within the various versions of apocalyptic worldview circulating during the New Testament era. Nevertheless, there are some things that are clear from the seeds of the prophetic tradition and the way these show up in the apocalyptic final judgment of the New Testament.

---

and consuming fire" (Isa. 30:30). Furthermore, Isaiah says about the wood in Topheth: "the breath of the Lord, like a stream of burning sulfur, sets it ablaze" (v. 33). The fire of Gehenna is not the source of evil, but it is from the Lord and is the end of evil.

James may not be suggesting anything differently from the pattern of Jeremiah 5:14. God's word in the mouth of Jeremiah will consume the people for the words they are speaking. If evil burns its course through our lives (like Isa. 33:11), the fire of Gehenna will then do its work (see Isa. 9:18–19). This reading of James 3:6 also fits with the warnings of Jesus that it is better to lose the part of ourselves that is doing evil than to have our whole body cast into Gehenna (Matt. 5:29–30; 18:9; Mark 9:43–47).

With all the evidence available to us, we can conclude that, in all biblical instances connecting Gehenna with judgment, Gehenna or the fire of Gehenna refer to the place in which the remains of the wicked are disposed—body and soul.

39. Ellens, "Afterlife and Underworld in the Bible," 4.

1) The wicked cannot avoid the judgment.
2) When the consequences come, they cannot be stopped, decreased, or reversed.
3) There are a variety of consequences commonly represented for the wicked.
    a) One is being cast out from the presence of God—darkness.[40]
    b) Death is certain.
    c) Any fire that follows will not fizzle, be dampened, or go out; it will destroy the remains of the wicked, body and soul.
4) There is no second chance or coming back from this judgment; it is final and total, all-consuming.
5) The righteous will have a place, be participants in, and be inheritors of the age to come; the wicked will not.
6) Only the righteous will be left in the transformed heavens and earth.

In the earliest traditions in the Scriptures, God's acts of judgment—however they come—utterly destroy the wicked, and the earth is cleansed of them (Gen. 19:23–29; Lev. 10:1–5; Num. 11:1–3; 16:35). It is difficult to make a case—although it is often done—that the prophets follow a perspective different than some form of annihilationism for the wicked. God's unquenchable, ever-vigilant fire accomplishes its cleansing work: "But who can endure the day of his coming? Who can stand when he appears? For he will be like a refiner's fire or a launderer's soap" (Mal. 3:2; see also Isa. 4:4; 26:11; Joel 2:3). Even though the smoke may

---

40. See the way John's Gospel speaks about the removal of sin and darkness in the process of delivering creation, rather than removing God's children from the wicked—as God did with Egypt in the book of Exodus (see Vail, "A New Exodus," in *Atonement and Salvation*, 63–76).

linger (Gen. 19:23–29; Ps. 37:20; Isa. 34:10; Rev. 14:11), the judgment need not take any time at all: "The Light of Israel will become a fire, their Holy One a flame; in a single day it will burn and consume his thorns and his briers" (Isa. 10:17; see vv. 16–18).

We have seen that in the transition to an apocalyptic worldview, in which there is eternal reward or punishment for what is done in this age, there were several different traditions that emerged about Sheol/Hades. One tradition, represented in Luke 16, divides the realm of the dead into sections for the righteous and the wicked. The wicked may be forever kept in that place and tormented, while the righteous are resurrected bodily for life in the age to come (like 1 Enoch 22:14). In the scriptural references to the Valley of Hinnom or Gehenna, there is no statement about eternal conscious torment, only the disposal of those already dead, which rids the land of them. On the heels of the New Testament era, that is not the case. Without any question, there are both Jewish and Christian writings after the New Testament era that turn Gehenna into a place of eternal conscious torment.

All of this is *not* to say that there are not texts in the canon from which we can make a case for eternal conscious torment; Revelation 14:9–11 and 20:10 are prime examples.[41] Jesus's statements in Matthew about the wicked being thrown outside into the darkness where there is "weeping and gnashing of teeth" can also go in the direction of eternal conscious torment—but not one connected directly to fire (8:12; 22:13; 25:30). The Scriptures do not give us a single, straightforward picture.

41. These too are debated. The apocalyptic genre of literature certainly needs to be handled responsibly no matter which interpretation a person takes.

The ultimate fate of the wicked has been a point of hot and, at times, ugly debate.[42] *First,* the debate has not been helped by the diverse views represented in the Bible by the transitions in perspective and differences in traditions. There is not only one perspective in our canon.

Second, after the New Testament era, traditions that emerged just before and during the New Testament era took off. Detailed theories about people being divided immediately at death into separate places of either paradise or torment increased in popularity; these went beyond what is represented in 1 Enoch 22 and Luke 16. Also, the notion of conscious, eternal torment for the wicked following final judgment eventually became the dominant position. Christian writings through the centuries detailing the eternal places of reward and punishment won the imaginations of Christians.

Third, the debate over the destiny of the wicked has not been helped by the way that the Greek terms "Hades" and "Gehenna" started to be translated as "hell" at the time of the Reformation. Centuries of Christian tradition shaped not only the way Scripture was read but also eventually the way it was translated. From the sixteenth and seventeenth centuries, Luther's translation of both "Hades" and "Gehenna" as *Hölle* and the King James Version translating them as "hell" made it even more difficult for Protestants to see the

---

42. In 2011, Rob Bell's book *Love Wins: A Book about Heaven, Hell, and the Fate of Every Person Who Ever Lived* (New York: HarperOne) created quite a stir. Nevertheless, books debating the fate of the wicked were available well before Bell's book. Here are just a few examples: William Crockett, ed., *Four Views on Hell* (Grand Rapids: Zondervan, 1992); Jonathan L. Kvanvig, *The Problem of Hell* (New York: Oxford University Press, 1993); David George Moore, *The Battle for Hell: A Survey and Evaluation of Evangelicals' Growing Attraction to the Doctrine of Annihilationism* (New York: University Press of America, Inc., 1995); Edward William Fudge and Robert A. Peterson, *Two Views of Hell: A Biblical & Theological Dialogue* (Downers Grove, IL: InterVarsity Press, 2000).

nuances of the biblical worldview and to avoid inserting later Christian developments into their reading of the Bible.[43]

Here is the bottom line. If we take what we have in our Scriptures—our rule for all matters of faith and doctrine—we have multiple, contrasting theologies. We should not pick only one biblical voice as the only or final word that counts on what the wicked will or will not experience. Across the history of Christianity, belief in eternal, conscious torment for the wicked is long and strong. Yet we should not break fellowship with one another by siding with that one perspective in the Bible and denouncing the others (and those who recognize them).

The point of judgment—the reason why it is hopeful in the midst of our present sufferings—is that wickedness will be eradicated from God's good creation. Judgment is consequence: bad news for the wicked but salvation to the righteous. So indeed, "Let all creation rejoice before the Lord, for he comes, he comes to judge the earth. He will judge the world in righteousness and the peoples in his faithfulness" (Ps. 96:13). For the sake of Christian unity, it might be better for us all to embrace the irreconcilable tensions in the Scriptures. That would mean embracing a certain humility that we do not know for certain exactly what will become of the wicked. The only consistency given on the issue in the Bible is that they will have no part or place in the life of the world to come. The final judgment is the final word for the wicked, with everlasting results. We should keep unity within the common confession of the

---

43. Ellens, "Afterlife and Underworld in the Bible," 5. As Ellens says it himself, "Both of these influential translations moralize the term hell as a place of the punishment of the wicked, thus radically changing the original thrust of the authentic biblical terms Sheol and Hades, and hence distorting severely the true meaning of the biblical text." See also Helsel's specific examples of passages where "hell" replaced the biblical terms in the KJV ("Hades, Hell, and Sheol," 109–11).

Christian faith: "He will come again in glory to judge the living and the dead."

Concerning the Righteous

A growing number of books have been written in recent decades about our ultimate home for all eternity. They are calling for us to look again at what the Scriptures actually say about the world and about heaven.[44] When we look closely, it may surprise us what we find in Scripture that doesn't align with our commonly held cultural beliefs. The contrast between common belief and the Scriptures is illustrated, for instance, by N. T. Wright.

"Traditionally," as Wright says, "we suppose that Christianity teaches about a heaven above, to which the saved or blessed go, and a hell below, for the wicked and impenitent."[45] Largely, however, "there is very little in the Bible about 'going to heaven when you die.'"[46] There is far more about God's kingdom or reign coming, the resurrection of the

---

44. As J. Richard Middleton explains this trend: "Over the past quarter of a century various evangelical Christian voices have articulated the bold, even startling, theological claim that the eternal destiny of the redeemed consists in the renewal of earthly life, to the exclusion of a disembodied heaven hereafter. This claim goes beyond the traditional, hybrid idea that we will experience eternal fellowship with God 'in heaven,' conceived as a non-physical realm, through the medium of a resurrected body. Indeed, this claim does away entirely with the notion of 'heaven' as an eternal hope, since this notion is thought to be fundamentally incompatible with authentic biblical faith" ("A New Heaven and a New Earth: The Case for a Holistic Reading of the Biblical Story of Redemption," *Journal for Christian Theological Research* 11 [2006]: 73, http://www2.luthersem.edu/ctrf/JCTR/Vol11/Middleton_vol11.pdf). See especially pages 73–77 and 86–97. A few recommended books include Barbara R. Rossing, *The Rapture Exposed: The Message of Hope in the Book of Revelation* (New York: Basic Books, 2005); N. T. Wright, *Surprised by Hope: Rethinking Heaven, the Resurrection, and the Mission of the Church* (New York: Harper One, 2008); J. Richard Middleton, *A New Heaven and a New Earth: Reclaiming Biblical Eschatology* (Grand Rapids: Baker Academic, 2014).

45. Wright, *Surprised by Hope*, 17.

46. Wright, *Surprised by Hope*, 18.

dead, making heaven and earth new, God coming to dwell on the earth, and the descent of the New Jerusalem to earth.[47] What will happen to human beings lies within the bigger picture of what God is doing for God's beloved creation. To restate Wright, *God is going to do for the whole cosmos what God did for Jesus at Easter.*[48] "The whole world is waiting on tiptoe with expectation, for the moment when that resurrection life and power sweeps through it, filling it with the glory of God as the waters cover the sea."[49] The glory of God's kingdom began to be at hand on earth in Christ's first coming: in breaking down social divides, correcting misunderstandings, feeding the hungry, healing bodies, casting out demons, teaching, and raising the dead. Jesus "was not saving souls for a disembodied eternity but rescuing people from the corruption and decay of the way the world presently is so they could enjoy, already in the present, that renewal of creation which is God's ultimate purpose."[50]

The Scriptures and earliest Christian teachings tie together our human destiny of resurrection life with the destiny of creation being redeemed. The salvation of *earthlings* requires the salvation of the *earth* (just as the land needs us to be set right). We are sixth-day land creatures. Our renewal necessitates the renewal of the place to which we are tied in substance, sustenance, habitation, and vocation. Recent studies of the Bible are getting us back in touch with its teachings. The renewed thinking about the destiny of the righteous is affirmed by the Nicene Creed, which correctly summarizes the scriptural perspective: "we look for the resurrection of the dead *and* the life of the world to come"

---

47. Wright, *Surprised by Hope*, 18–19.
48. Wright, *Surprised by Hope*, 93; see also 80.
49. Wright, *Surprised by Hope*, 108.
50. Wright, *Surprised by Hope*, 192.

(emphasis added). The claims before and after the "and" must be included in our theology.

My whole life I have heard from some believers the affirmation that "this world is not our home," taken to mean that we will spend eternity somewhere else. This view misses the New Testament usage of "the world" to describe the way God's good creation is operating in this age under the shadows of sin and death (John 1:9–10; 3:16–17; 4:42; 7:7; 12:47; 16:33; 17:13–21; 1 John 2:15–17). In many instances "the world" does not mean this beloved creation of God, over which God has faithfully labored from the dawn of time. We certainly are to have no part in the sinful patterns of "the world" in this age. That does not mean we will not remain in the world, both now and in the life of the world to come. Christ is the Savior of the world (John 3:17; 4:42) who "takes away the sin of the world" (1:29) and drives out "the prince of this world" (12:31). Truly, our Christian hope and confession is that we look for "the renewal of all things" (Matt. 19:28). We are even now experiencing tastes of the age to come and living under the lordship of the King of kings, whose kingdom will have no end. God's kingdom has been coming and will continue to come until it fully arrives at Christ's return.

With our confusion about "the world" comes our confusion about the place of heaven in the Scriptures. The final verses of many hymns in our hymnals talk about going to heaven for eternity and what that will be like. That is upside down from the renewal taught by the prophets, which follows judgment and the purging of wickedness. In that renewal, the people and land will be arranged with God present at the heart of it all. Indeed, the book of Ezekiel ends with the naming of the central place in the land: "THE LORD IS THERE" (48:35). It is always the holy ones who will participate in God's renewing blessings—whether those are periods of renewal in history or the ultimate making new of the heavens and the earth for the age to come. This makes Jesus's promise in the Beatitudes so potent: "Blessed are the meek, for they will inherit the earth" (Matt. 5:5).

In some belief systems that view heaven as our destiny, it is viewed "as a mystical place in the clouds with an unending church service."[51] Even if not that precise image, it is believed our deceased loved ones are immediately and forevermore taken there at the moment of death. Even though there is no resurrection in that view, it gives people comfort in their grief that their Christian brother or sister is 'in heaven' or 'a better place'; our loss is their gain. Certainly Luke's Gospel refers to the place we await the resurrection as "paradise" (23:43; see also 16:22). We also have comfort from Paul's letters that, in death, we remain in Christ and cannot be separated from God.

The Scriptures indeed give us assurances in our grief for the comfort and safekeeping of our loved ones. These are just different assurances than the common narratives about heaven. The Scriptures also give us a posture in which to stand in the face of death that neither embraces nor absolutizes it; instead we say: *Death, you will not have the final word here!* This all means, however, that whatever state our loved ones enter at death is not everlasting. There is not a single New Testament book that contradicts the teaching that the dead will be resurrected at Christ's return. Heaven, or any other interim resting place, is never named as our eternal home in the Scriptures.

Heaven has a different function in Scripture. Heaven itself is not eternal but a part of God's creation; "In the beginning God created the heavens and the earth" (Gen. 1:1; see also Col. 1:16). In the ancient world, "heaven" is

---

51. Paul Enns, *Heaven Revealed* (Chicago: Moody Publishers, 2011), 18.

considered to be everything above the ground: the atmosphere, the place of the sun, moon, and stars, and the realm in which God fully dwells. Since it starts right above the ground, anywhere a person goes on the earth, heaven is present.[52] It is present without being limited to one spot. It is, thus, the perfect place from which to govern. This is why the resurrected and victorious Christ ascended to God's heavenly throne (Phil. 2:9–11; Rev. 1:12–18; 5:5–14) and "the ruler of the kingdom of the air" loses his grip (Eph. 2:1–9; John 12:31). Thus, Christ "is both already ruling the rebellious present world as its rightful Lord and also interceding for us at the Father's right hand."[53]

In the structure of creation, heaven is God's throne, and the earth is God's footstool (Isa. 66:1; Acts 7:49). "The Lord has established his throne in heaven, and his kingdom rules over all" (Ps. 103:19). In Matthew's Gospel, Jesus gives the image of heaven not only as being God's throne, but God also sits on it (Matt. 23:22; see also Matt. 5:34; Rev. 4:2).[54] In this arrangement, God is observant of all that goes on in creation (Ps. 11:4; see also Isa. 63:15). Around

---

52. Wright, *Surprised by Hope*, 111. It may be helpful for contemporary thinkers to hear Wright's further explanation about heaven: "when the Bible speaks of heaven and earth it is not talking about two localities related to each other within the same space-time continuum or about a nonphysical world contrasted with a physical one but about two different kinds of what we call space, two different kinds of what we call matter, and also quite possible (though this does not necessarily follow from the other two) two different kinds of what we call time" (115). Wright recommends that we regain our imagination about C. S. Lewis's Narnia, which is related and interlocked with earth. "God's space and ours interlock and intersect in a whole variety of ways even while they retain, for the moment at least, their separate and distinct identities and roles" (116).

53. Wright, *Surprised by Hope*, 113.

54. We should not miss, however, that the tabernacle and temple were a special touchpoint between heaven and earth. The holy of holies in no way contained God (1 Kings 8:13, 27; 2 Chron. 6:2, 18). Nevertheless, within that special touchpoint between heaven and earth, God "is enthroned between the cherubim on the ark" (2 Sam. 6:2; see also 1 Sam. 4:4; 1 Chron. 13:6; Exod. 25:22; Num. 7:89). In the New Testament, the imagery and function of the temple are

the Lord are gathered the "multitudes of heaven" (1 Kings 22:19; 2 Chron. 18:18; Rev. 5:13). As God is enthroned there, God's will and reign are realized in heaven, and we ought to pray for their full realization on earth (Matt. 6:10), even as God's kingdom is already coming (Mark 1:15). All of this points to the structuring of God's creation with heaven and earth.

In the ordering of the cosmos, all blessings flow from God our heavenly Father, in Christ, by the Holy Spirit, as God's life-fostering reign unfolds in the midst of the earth's bondage under sin and death. The movement is from heaven to earth. The blessings of God pour out from heaven upon the earth to renew and bring life to the earth and its inhabitants (Acts 14:17). A quick survey of "heaven" in the New Testament illustrates this. In John's Gospel, for instance, there are seventeen verses in which the word "heaven" appears. John says things come "down from heaven" eight times (1:32; 6:33, 38, 41, 42, 50, 51, 58) and says that things are "from heaven" seven times (3:13, 27, 31; 6:31, 32; 12:28). In the other few references, he says something is "heavenly" (3:12), Jesus "looked to heaven" (17:1), we will see "heaven open" (1:51), and only the Son of Man "has ever gone into heaven" (3:13). John never says *we* will go there.

It is common to read "heaven" into Jesus's pre-crucifixion statement in John 14:1–4: "Do not let your hearts be troubled. You believe in God; believe also in me. My Father's house has many rooms; if that were not so, would I have told you that I am going there to prepare a place for you? And if I go and prepare a place for you, I will come back and take you to be with me that you also may be where I am. You know the way to the place where I am going."

---

transferred to Jesus. This becomes explicit in Revelation 21:22: "I did not see a temple in the city, because the Lord God Almighty and the Lamb are its temple."

When Thomas asks *where* Jesus is going so he can know the way (v. 5), Jesus says he is talking about our coming *to the Father* through himself (vv. 6–7). The emphasis of John's Gospel is the abiding of the Father in the Son and the Son in the Father (vv. 9–11) and the gathering of Christ's followers into abiding in fellowship with the Father, Son, and Spirit. As Gail O'Day writes in her commentary, "This reference to the Father's house needs to be read first in the context of the mutual indwelling of God and Jesus, a form of 'residence' that has been repeatedly stressed from the opening verses of the Gospel (e.g., 1:1, 18). Throughout the Gospel, location has consistently been a symbol for relationship."[55]

The whole of chapter 14 explains this. The Spirit will abide in believers (v. 17; see also 3:5–8), and Christ will abide in them (v. 20), even as Christ himself is in the Father (v. 20), to whom he is going (vv. 2–3, 12). For believers, there will be no loss of abiding by Christ's going; in fact, through his death, resurrection, and ascension we are gathered into that abiding through Christ. There is a reciprocity of Christ being in them and them being in Christ (v. 20; see also John 6). This shared fellowship with the Father, Son, and Spirit is the basis of the believers coming to God (14:6), knowing God (vv. 7, 9, 17), being able to petition the Father in Jesus's name (vv. 13–14), doing great works (v. 12), and following Jesus's commands (vv. 15, 21, 23). In Christ's movement through the cross, resurrection, and ascension, we are gathered into communion with God. Christ is going to prepare space for us in the amply spacious household of the Father.[56] John 14:1–4 is not a statement about us going

---

55. O'Day, *The Gospel of John*, 740.

56. As O'Day says, "room" in 14:2 is related to the verb "remain" or "to dwell" (741). The verb form of the noun is "used in the Fourth Gospel to describe the mutuality and reciprocity of the relationship of God and Jesus (14:10; 15:10).

to heaven. Rather, in all the clarifications that follow, the movement is toward fellowship with God. It ends in divine coming: "Anyone who loves me will obey my teaching. My Father will love them, and we will come to them and make our home with them" (v. 23).

The good news is that the earth has been blessed with divine life in the Son's incarnation and by the outworking of the Holy Spirit (Matt. 12:28; Luke 4:1, 14, 18–19). The double stitch of divine life infilling the earth and earth inhabiting divine fellowship is then completed in Christ's ascension (John 14:1–14, 20–23; 20:17). The life of heaven and earth—Creator and creature—are sown together (Eph. 1:9–10; Col. 1:20). There is reciprocal indwelling; we are being infilled in Christ (John 6:53; 14:17, 20), and we are abiding in the Lord (John 6:56; 14:20; 15:5–7; 17:21–23). Even the distinction between the realms of heaven and earth start to get blurred through the ministry of Christ. The heavens open, or are torn open, at Christ's baptism; the blessings of the kingdom of heaven break into earthly life by the Spirit. Also, in Christian worship, through Christ, believers enter before the heavenly throne of God (Heb. 9:24; 10:19–22).[57]

At Christ's second coming, the ultimate "times of refreshing" will "come from the Lord" (Acts 3:19). But "heaven must receive [Christ] until the time comes for God to restore everything, as he promised long ago through his holy prophets" (v. 21; see Isa. 65:17; 66:12; 2 Thess. 2:8; 1 Pet. 3:22; 4:13; 5:1, 4, 10). Jesus says this restoration will happen when the Father and Son "come to them and make [their] home with them" (John 14:23; see v. 28), joining the

---

The use of this noun here (see also 14:23) points to the inclusion of others in this relationship, this 'house'" (741).

57. See Alexander Schmemann, "The Eucharist," in *For the Life of the World* (Crestwood, NY: St. Vladimir's Seminary Press, 1963), 23–46.

already indwelling Spirit (v. 17). The *coming* of our Savior from heaven will "bring everything under his control," and he "will transform our lowly bodies so that they will be like his glorious body" (Phil. 3:21; see 1 Thess. 1:10; 1 Pet. 1:3–5; 1 John 3:2). God is preparing "in heaven" (2 Cor. 5:1) the type of transformed bodily existence that Paul calls "our heavenly dwelling" (vv. 2, 4). But these will come to clothe us, and thus our mortality will be swallowed up by life (vv. 2, 4). Along with these blessings of transformation, there are even treasures or a reward being stored up "in heaven" that we can receive at that time (Matt. 5:12; 6:19–20; 19:21).

Whether the New Testament says Jesus "comes," "is revealed" (1 Cor. 1:7–8; 2 Thess. 1:7; 1 Pet. 1:3–5, 13), "descends" (Acts 1:11), or "appears" (Col. 3:4; 1 Tim. 6:14; 2 Tim. 4:8; Titus 2:11–14; Heb. 9:28; 1 Pet. 5:4; 1 John 2:28; 3:2), he is going to bring *from heaven* the kind of restoration depicted in the prophets, which means full and final "salvation to those who are waiting for him" (Heb. 9:28). In Christ, heaven and earth are so stitched together that any discernible boundary distinctions between them will utterly blur in the age to come. N. T. Wright calls this cosmic transformation at Christ's return "the marriage of heaven and earth."[58] Rather than being seated in heaven, God's dwelling will be entirely and forevermore among us.

The Scriptures move in the direction of God coming, not us going. This was one of Martin Luther's great breakthroughs in reading the Scriptures in the time of the Reformation. He warned Christians that they mistakenly had been reversing the gospel into a story of human ascent and glorification when, in fact, the gospel is a story of God's descent: "The kingdom of God has come near. Repent and

---

58. Wright, *Surprised by Hope*, 104.

believe the good news!" (Mark 1:15).[59] This is a reminder Christians need to receive in every generation. Christians do not believe in escaping the world or in shedding our bodies; we look for earth to receive its King and the life of the world to come.

Some of the previous chapters in this book have been looking at the narrative arc of the Scriptures and the hope of Christ's return here, the sorting of all people (the living and the dead), the elimination of all agents of destruction in the world, the transformation of all things, and the everlasting reign of God. As a result, the claims being made in this section should not come as a surprise. However, there are a few biblical texts that can potentially create uncertainty or confusion. First Thessalonians 4 might be top among those.

Paul was writing to the Thessalonian church, in part, to ease their distress that some members were dying before Christ's return. They were concerned that the dead were not going to participate in the coming reign of their King. They were grieving the deaths of their Christian brothers and sisters as people without hope (1 Thess. 4:13). Here is what Paul tells them in vv. 14–18 to set their theology straight:

> For we believe that Jesus died and rose again, and so we believe that God will bring with Jesus those who have fallen asleep in him. According to the Lord's word, we tell you that we who are still alive, who are left until the coming of the Lord, will certainly not precede those who have fallen asleep. For the Lord himself will come down from heaven, with a loud command, with the voice of the archangel and with the trumpet call of God, and the dead in Christ will rise first. After that, we who are still alive and are left

---

59. See, for example, his *Heidelberg Disputations*, 19–21, http://www.bookof-concord.org/heidelberg.php.

will be caught up together with them in the clouds to meet the Lord in the air. And so we will be with the Lord forever. Therefore encourage one another with these words.

This description of Christ's return includes the words "rise," "caught up together," "in the clouds," and "in the air" (vv. 16–17). There is no wonder that this has created confusion for readers that somehow we will be whisked away to heaven forever.

It is important with any text to make sure we are not losing something through translation or unfamiliar cultural practices, and this is a text that has been tragically misread for both reasons. English readers hear that all these things are going to happen at "the coming of the Lord" (v. 15). We miss that Paul has actually said this is "the *parousia* of the Lord." A *parousia* is an event in the Greco-Roman world that Paul did not need to explain to his audience. They would have known how a *parousia* unfolds, just as most people today know how a parade unfolds without being told. When we hear the time and route of a parade, we know we are not supposed to march the route ourselves or stand in the middle of the street. We know that our role as spectators is to line the route. A *parousia* is a bit like that. The most classic example we have of a *parousia* in the New Testament is Palm Sunday, when Jesus was hailed by the masses as they ushered him into Jerusalem. In the Greco-Roman world, if people in a town heard the cry of heralds or the sounding of trumpets that an important person was coming, they would go out of the city, line the pathway, and gladly receive the person and the honor the person's presence brought to their town. At the front of the town's reception, they would always place their highest-ranking people in order to show due respect to the approaching figure. Through this process, the citizens "received" the guest; they did not go somewhere else.

With all of these clarifications about Paul's description of Christ's *parousia*, 1 Thessalonians 4 sounds so much different. First, this congregation thought dead people were going to be left out—since people who die in *this* age miss out on what comes next *in this age*. So, Paul starts in verse 14 with the assurance that, just as Jesus died and rose again, their dead members will also rise again to participate in the festivities of the age to come. In fact, Paul quickly clarifies that those who have gone to the grave still continuing in their faithfulness to the Lord will be among the highest ranked in the processional: "we who are still alive, who are left until the coming of the Lord, will certainly not precede those who have fallen asleep" (v. 15). With those assurances that the dead will participate and be first among us, Paul describes the *parousia* itself.

The Lord is going to be coming down from heaven (v. 16). That is an appropriate expectation, given what the disciples were told at Jesus's ascension: "This same Jesus, who has been taken from you into heaven, will come back in the same way you have seen him go into heaven" (Acts 1:11). His coming will be heralded "with the voice of the archangel and with the trumpet call of God" (1 Thess. 4:16); we will hear it! At the announcement, our most important people will lead our greeting party; "the dead in Christ will rise first" (v. 16). The less noble people follow them; "we who are still alive and are left will be caught up together with them in the clouds to meet the Lord in the air" (v. 17). Since Jesus will not be traveling by way of a road along the ground, the only way to line his route of return is for us to be caught up. Paul never says in 1 Thessalonians 4:17 where "we will be with the Lord forever." He did not have to tell his Greek-speaking audience the location because they knew that, at a *parousia,* they were ushering very important people into their own midst.

No Greek reader would have misunderstood Paul the way English readers do because of our language and cultural barriers. So long as we understand that Paul is describing an event like Jesus being welcomed into Jerusalem on Palm Sunday, we cannot miss it. Jesus is coming to our home forever! And anyone who has died "in Christ" will be included in that! "Therefore encourage one another with these words" (v. 18).

We should not be disappointed in the life of the world to come—as if we are being robbed of heaven. The fullness of God and all the blessings of the kingdom of heaven will be coming down. "Look! God's dwelling place is now among the people, and he will dwell with them. They will be his people, and God himself will be with them and be their God" (Rev. 21:3). We will see face to face (1 Cor. 13:12). The old order of things will pass away (Rev. 21:4). Everything about life in the world will be transformed as it is swallowed up in divine life. God will be all in all, and all things will be ordered unto the glory of God. This will be life to the full—eternal life. It is the very life we are already tasting as we live by the very same Spirit who raised Christ from the dead. What a day that will be—a day without end!

SEVEN

Heeding Revelation Today

John, To the seven churches in the province of Asia: Grace and peace to you from him who is, and who was, and who is to come, and from the seven spirits before his throne, and from Jesus Christ, who is the faithful witness, the firstborn from the dead, and the ruler of the kings of the earth. To him who loves us and has freed us from our sins by his blood, and has made us to be a kingdom and priests to serve his God and Father—to him be glory and power for ever and ever! Amen.

—*Revelation 1:4–6*

Then I heard another voice from heaven say: "'Come out of [Babylon], my people,' so that you will not share in her sins, so that you will not receive any of her plagues; for her sins are piled up to heaven, and God has remembered her crimes."

—*Revelation 18:4–5*

As a child I remember attending one performance of Handel's *Messiah*, and sadly, it required more attention than I could muster at the time. It was not until I participated in choir during my freshman year of college that Dr. Marvin Stallcop helped me fall in love with the greatness of Handel's work. We saw the work come alive before us as Dr. Stallcop directed with the bounce, sway, or tensing of his whole body. His facial expressions conveyed to us the sentiment of every word he wanted us to emote. Not only did we learn to inhabit the movement and feeling of the music, but we also learned to pay attention to the words as we enunciated them for the audience.

Messiah is a masterpiece in musical composition—setting the words of Scripture to music in a way that perfectly elevates them. Two choruses among the greats are the "Hallelujah Chorus," for which audiences still stand, and "Worthy is the Lamb." Both songs declare, at full voice, uncontestable praise to our Lord. The repeated swelling of hallelujahs, declarations of highest titles, and worthiness of the Lamb as the one who was slain are all sung with as much force as the human body can muster. Even now I am so thankful each year to be able to join the chorus of voices at Mount Vernon Nazarene University in singing these scriptures! It feels like heaven and earth unite as we worship in singing *Messiah*.

It was not until my years singing at MVNU that I paid attention to *where* the lyrics of *Messiah* are found in the Bible. The two thunderous choruses I mentioned come from the book of Revelation.

- "Then I heard what sounded like a great multitude, like the roar of rushing waters and like loud peals of thunder, shouting: 'Hallelujah! For our Lord God Almighty reigns'" (Rev. 19:6).

- "The seventh angel sounded his trumpet, and there were loud voices in heaven, which said: 'The kingdom of the world has become the kingdom of our Lord and of his Messiah, and he will reign for ever and ever'" (Rev. 11:15).

- "On his robe and on his thigh he has this name written: KING OF KINGS AND LORD OF LORDS" (Rev. 19:16).

- "In a loud voice they were saying: 'Worthy is the Lamb, who was slain, to receive power and wealth and wisdom and strength and honor and glory and praise!' Then I heard every creature in heaven and on earth and under the earth and on the sea, and all that is in them, saying: 'To him who sits on the throne and to the Lamb be praise and honor and glory and power, for ever and ever!'" (Rev. 5:12–13). How can it be that the book of the Bible that exhausts every molecule of our breath in singing its words of praise to God can also be the book that most terrifies many believers?

The Landscape of Revelation

The worshipful attitude of Revelation is often obscured by its larger-than-life fantastical imagery. What are we to make of beasts and circumstances beyond anything humans have experienced on earth? While we have had localized or regional wars and catastrophes, we have no historical comparison to waves of planet-wide devastation that would kill a quarter of the whole earth's population (6:8) or destroy a third of all the trees, plants, the sea, sea creatures, rivers, springs, and the remainder of humankind (8:7–12; 9:18).[1] Also, except for the help of Hollywood special effects, none of us has ever seen anything like six-winged creatures (4:8), a seven-headed dragon (12:3), or the two other beasts described in the book (13:1, 11).

While on one hand Revelation can seem disorienting, unclear, or beyond reality, on the other hand, it is quite simple. It depicts a clear, two-sided division in the world: good and bad, God and Satan, truth and lies, the church and Babylon, faithful and unfaithful, separation and participation, salvation and destruction. As with all of Scripture, there is the path of *life* and the path of *death* (see Deut.

---

1. See Bauckham, *Theology of the Book of Revelation.*

30:19–20).[2] With only two clear-cut sides, that makes the book as simple as a person could hope for.

The Triune God in Revelation

On the one side is the category of the one, true, triune God—the Father, Son, and Holy Spirit. Of all the grand imagery Revelation offers, the first in line is the exalted Christ and the image of the throne room of God (1, 4, 5). In order to see all things in the world correctly, readers must first have their eyes calibrated with the One who is Truth (our Beginning and End), and is thus the criteria for what is true and false in the world. We see in these chapters an ever-larger choir singing the praises of God and the Lamb, to the point that "every creature" comes to praise the Lamb (4:8, 10–11; 5:8–10, 11–12, 13–14). We see at the start that this is the right order of all things. God is at the front and center of the whole revelation.

The arrangement of God's throne room puts the throne of God at the center, with all things encircling it in an ordered manner. This circular gathering is similar to the way God asked the twelve tribes of Israel to camp around God's tabernacle in the forty years of desert wandering (Num. 2; see also Ezek. 40–48). The number of elders arrayed around God's throne in Revelation 4–5 is twenty-four. To the elders of Israel's twelve tribes (Num. 1:44) have been added the twelve apostles of Jesus (see Luke 22:28–30; Acts 1:12–26). Together the twenty-four elders on their thrones represent the covenant people of God from each of the two Testaments. There are also representatives of living creatures (Rev. 4:6–7) who lead ceaseless praise of God (v. 8) in which the elders join (vv. 9–11). This image is how all of life ought to be ordered, if God's will is to be done on earth as it is in heaven.

---

2. My thanks to Rick Williamson for connecting the two sides of Revelation with the broader scriptural contrast between life and death.

It also clarifies that, at the heart of the cosmos, in spite of the dysfunctions we experience day to day, God is already and always enthroned. God alone is the holy, everlasting One (v. 8) who is ultimately worthy of all glory, honor, and power as our Creator (v. 11).

Revelation 5 shows that in God's right hand (the hand of God's power) is a sealed scroll.[3] No one in heaven or on earth was worthy to open or look at this scroll concerning God's exercise of power (5:3–4).[4] But John is told to look at the triumphant Lion of Judah who can unlock for us God's power (v. 5). It certainly sounds appropriate that the Lion should be connected to divine power. When John obeys what he *hears* and looks at the already victorious Lion, he *sees* a freshly slaughtered Lamb (v. 6) encircled by the heavenly worshipers. The triumphant Lion, precisely as the slain Lamb, is the one who is "worthy to take the scroll" from God's right hand "and open its seals" (v. 9). It is in the power of the Son's own sacrifice that "the true meaning of power, judgment, and salvation" is manifest.[5] Christ crucified is the power of God (1 Cor. 1:18). Being one with the Father, the Son opens the scroll of divine power: in that "you were slain, and with your blood you purchased for God persons from every tribe and language and people and nation. You have made them to be a kingdom and priests to serve our God, and they will reign on the earth" (Rev. 5:9–10; see also Exod. 19:4–6; 1 Pet. 2:9–10).

If readers miss this opening image of God, which connects divine power with the victory won in Christ laying

---

3. This is also the hand with which God offers blessing and reassurance (Rev. 1:17).

4. Michael J. Gorman, *Reading Revelation Responsibly: Uncivil Worship and Witness: Following the Lamb into the New Creation* (Eugene, OR: Cascade Books, 2011), 109, 111, see also footnote 15 on 109.

5. Gorman, *Reading Revelation Responsibly*, 110.

Revelation clearly shows that the Lion won victory through Calvary, as the slaughtered Lamb.

down his own life to liberate people "to be a kingdom and priests" (Rev. 5:10), the rest of the book will be misread. God wields power in self-sacrificing, other-nurturing love. Nothing about that has changed from the dawn of creation to the age to come; it is our beginning and end. If we have seen the Son, we have seen the Father (John 14:9); the Son does only what he sees the Father doing (John 5:19; see v. 36). There is no other kind of divine power than what we see in the Son bearing wounds to reconcile even God's own enemies (Rom. 5:12; Col. 1:19–21). Revelation clearly shows that the Lion won victory through Calvary, as the slaughtered Lamb. Paul concurs with John's vision: "having disarmed the powers and authorities, he made a public spectacle of them, triumphing over them by the cross" (Col. 2:15). The cross may be utter "foolishness to those who are perishing, but to us who are being saved it is the power of God" (1 Cor. 1:18).

The third Person of the Trinity is the Spirit. Christ is the very message of the Spirit. As the letters to the seven churches show, the message of the book is about Christ and from Christ, while at the same time they are to "hear what the Spirit says to the churches" (Rev. 2:7, 11, 17, 29; 3:6, 13, 22). The Spirit conveys the message; the Spirit should be heard. John himself is "in the Spirit" (4:2; 17:3; 21:10) while this revelation from and about Christ is conveyed. It is difficult to separate out being caught up in the Messenger (Spirit) from participation in the Message (Christ).[6] This

---

6. References to the Holy Spirit are a difficult component in interpreting Revelation. John uses "Spirit" (1:10; 2:7, 11, 17, 29; 3:6, 13, 22; 4:2; 14:13; 17:3; 19:10; 21:10; 22:17) and "seven spirits" (1:4; 3:1; 4:5; 5:6). Bauckham suggests, "The seven Spirits should be understood as a symbol for the divine Spirit, which John has chosen on the basis of his exegesis of Zechariah 4:1–14" (*Theology of the Book of Revelation*, 110). The number seven is a symbol associated with completeness and perfection. "The seven Spirits are the fullness of God's power 'sent out into all the earth' (5:6). . . . The seven Spirits are closely associated with

central vision of the Holy Trinity must calibrate our reading of everything in Revelation.

Revelation's Dark Triad

On the other side in Revelation we find Satan's unholy triad—along with Satan the dragon (12:3–13:11; 20:2) are the sea beast of the empire (13:1–10) and the land beast, the advocate for Satan's sea beast (13:11–18). Everything said about this satanic triad is a parody of the Father, Son, and Holy Spirit. For example, just as the Lamb sits on the throne with the Father and forever is given praise, honor, glory, and power (5:12–13), so also "the dragon gave the beast his power and his throne and great authority" (13:2). Even though the beast's names and prideful claims were blasphemous against the slain Lamb (13:1, 5–6), people worshiped and followed the beast out of wonder for its predatory physique (13:2–3) and its unchallengeable power in warfare (13:4, 7, 10). People show wonder—"Who is like the beast?" (13:4)—that should only be exclaimed in response to God (Exod. 15:11; Ps. 35:10; 71:19).[7]

In all ways, the beast is a blasphemous counterpoint to the slaughtered Lamb whose own blood was poured out for the sake of others. This agent of Satan in Revelation is the Roman Empire and its ungodly power dynamics. The

the victorious Lamb (5:6): the four references to them indicate that the Lamb's victory is implemented throughout the world by the fullness of divine power" (109). It is not that there are nine persons of the Trinity: the Father, Son, and seven spirits. Rather, there is a sevenfold manner of the Spirit's activity; it is perfect and complete. Revelation shows us that God and the Lamb are enthroned at the center of all things—the Lamb is victorious—and the phrase "seven spirits" places the Holy Spirit together with them in the completeness of God's triune dominion. The four references to "seven spirits" occur in the first five chapters, in which Revelation is calibrating readers' vision of God and the true ordering of the cosmos.

7. David A. DeSilva, *Unholy Allegiances: Heeding Revelation's Warning* (Peabody, MA: Hendrickson Publishers, 2013), 45.

second beast from the land is an unholy counterpoint to the Holy Spirit. The land beast, as a false prophet (Rev. 16:13; 19:20), leads the earth's inhabitants to worship the sea beast (13:12) and dragon (13:4) "by deceit (19:20) and coercion (13:15–17)."[8] It fosters allegiance through routine messaging, cultural rituals, or force. All of the language and symbols of the empire "constructed a world in which inhabitants of Rome and the provinces lived, moved, and had their being."[9] All the empire's claims, monuments, and statues "constructed the entire cosmos in which Roman citizens lived."[10] While readers of Revelation are shown that the empire's self-narratives are lies, those living in the empire thought the sea beast gave them a true account of the cosmos and divine power.[11]

The book of Revelation works by exposing the truth about routine life. It takes mundane daily practices that every person in the Roman Empire would take for granted and shows they are not harmless, normal, acceptable, or positive. It enlarges little parts of normal life to monstrous scale so we can see their true character. It is like seeing the tiny face of a spider under intense magnification. That level of detail can cause nightmares. By magnifying mundane political, military, and economic activities to fantastic scale, Revelation shows that life in the empire is beastly, death-dealing, and shares Satan's throne.

---

8. Bauckham, *Theology of the Book of Revelation*, 115; see also 114.

9. Hansen, *Silence and Praise*, 52.

10. Hansen, *Silence and Praise*, 55.

11. "The dragon is the one who deceives the whole world (12:9; cf. 20:2–3, 7–8), the second beast deceives the inhabitants of the earth with its propaganda for the divinity of the beast (13:14; cf. 19:21), Babylon deceives all nations with her sorceries (18:23), but the followers of the Lamb, like the Lamb himself, are entirely without deceit (14:5; cf. 3:14)" (Bauckham, *Theology of the Book of Revelation*, 91).

An additional symbol in Revelation that is connected to the first beast (Rev. 13, 17) is the harlot (Rev. 17–18). The beast embodies power (the political and military side of empire), and the harlot embodies wealth—the economic side of the empire. The economic greatness of the harlot rides on the political and military practices of the beast (17:3). These are not merely secular, or religiously neutral, realms. Participation with the beast/harlot is inseparable from showing where one's religious allegiance and devotion lie.[12]

The two symbols of power and wealth represent Rome (called "Babylon" throughout the book) in enormously unflattering ways. When Revelation was written, Rome was the capital city of the dominant empire. Rome was often "celebrated as the source of prosperity for the whole world. The luxury of Rome was taken as a sign that a golden age of prosperity had returned to the entire Mediterranean world."[13] Rome was held to be divinely sanctioned as "a pillar for the stability and security of all peoples, tribes, nations, and languages."[14] They were praised for building infrastructure for land and sea travel, which aided the transportation of both commercial goods and essentials like food and water. They were known for viciously tamping down any uprisings among groups within their borders and for being too fearsome to challenge by outsiders. This brutally maintained quiet was celebrated as the *Pax Romana*—the peace of Rome.

With all the wealth and "peace and security" that it promised the world, a lore developed among Rome's ruling classes that the world had freely given them their power "by universal consent."[15] Public inscriptions placed across

---

12. Bauckham, *Theology of the Book of Revelation*, 36.
13. DeSilva, *Unholy Allegiances*, 24.
14. DeSilva, *Unholy Allegiances*, 35.
15. DeSilva, *Unholy Allegiances*, 25.

the empire by Augustus and his successors make the self-claim "of 'having obtained all things *by universal consent*,' and of being given the title '"Augustus" *by universal decree*.' Far from being a tyrant, this inscription claims, Augustus had greatness thrust upon him by universal acclaim, and appropriately so, given all he had done on behalf of the world."[16] They claimed that the world wanted Rome's rulers to expand the empire because—through its politics, military, and economics—it was offering *salvation* to the world. The consistent messaging of the empire was often successful; the land beast accomplished its job in service to the sea beast. All across history there are examples of dominating systems that succeed in indoctrinating "all participants, so that ongoing commitment to the system is assured even by those who are most disadvantaged by the system. They are also often accompanied by ideologies of self-aggrandizement, if not self-worship, that also serve to mask the costs of the systems in terms of human suffering and dignity."[17] The self-promotion of the empire finds its way into the hearts and onto the lips of its own victims.

In a strange twist, not everyone suffers under empires—especially those in the top ranks; also, some kings of the earth (17:2; 18:3) and merchants (18:3) give themselves over to the harlot in order to participate in her splendor. They can occasionally profit so long as they assist the empire in feeding its insatiable consumption. There was not a luxury item the harlot would not purchase, including human beings themselves (18:11–15). Cozying up to her may have given dealers the illusion of security, but the truth is that she drinks from her golden cup filled with abomina-

---

16. DeSilva, *Unholy Allegiances*, 25.
17. DeSilva, *Unholy Allegiances*, 109.

tions (17:2, 4)[18]—including being "drunk with the blood of God's holy people" (v. 6). She rides on the beast that crushes any who dare contend with it (v. 3). The ways she profits those at the top, at the expense of the masses, and corrupts the hearts and lives of everyone in the empire "rest on the power achieved and maintained by the imperial armies."[19]

The claim that Rome is freely given allegiance requires us never to mind the vast military resources they wield to seize, demand, and hold dominion, or its systems of economic exploitation for the advantage of the wealthy.[20] Unlike God, who works for the good of others (especially the least of these), Rome is self-interested. Unlike imaging God in tending and keeping God's good creation, Rome and its people are guilty of destroying God's sanctuary (11:18). The empire shows itself as one "whose influence and interventions ultimately seek to secure self-serving ends . . . as Rome is seen to consume more of the world's goods than any one city . . . and this often to the detriment of the provinces under her far-from-beneficent rule."[21] The world looks upon it and marvels at the grandeur of empire, believing it praiseworthy. They cannot help but think it surely must be backed by the gods (or God).[22] Revelation, however, opens the curtains on the truth about Rome; there is nothing god-

---

18. Bauckham, *Theology of the Book of Revelation*, 37.

19. Bauckham, *Theology of the Book of Revelation*, 36.

20. DeSilva, *Unholy Allegiances*, 65.

21. DeSilva, *Unholy Allegiances*, 67.

22. "It is one of the deepest ironies of Christian history that, when the Roman Empire became nominally Christian under the Christian emperors, Christianity came to function not so very differently from the state religion which Revelation portrays as Rome's idolatrous self-deification. The Christian emperor's rule was seen as an image of God's own sovereignty, and while this did include the notion of the emperor's responsibility to God, it also provided religious justification for absolute monarchy. However, this is the exact opposite of the way the image of divine sovereignty functions in Revelation. There, so far from legitimizing human autocracy, divine rule radically de-legitimizes it" (Bauckham, *Theology of the Book of Revelation*, 44).

ly, good, or praiseworthy about Satan's agent. Any wonder and praise for the beast (earthly empire) is actually worship of Satan "because he had given authority to the beast" (13:4).

Following the Trinity in Revelation

This satanic triad is such a stark contrast to the holy Trinity. This revelation exposes the dynamics of earthly kingdoms through larger-than-life, cartoonish imagery. On the other side it orients us in God's ways and how God's people are to live in the empire. Seeing the slaughtered Lamb helps us understand the scroll in God's right hand (see also Phil. 2:5–11). Importantly, the contents of the scroll are not the seals themselves.[23] As the seals of judgment are broken, everything in the world that follows Satan's deceptions experiences the consequence of living unlike the Lamb.[24] They are handed over to the deadly effects of their ways (see Rom. 1:18–32). In breaking the seals, God is not overpowering Caesar in a violent takeover, in the way that worldly kingdoms seize and hold power.[25] *God is seeking to redeem Babylon while all of the promises of their worldview unravel. God's goal and hope are that they might repent.*[26] The worldly order of Rome is shown for what it is (of Satan) and how it does not comply with the power of God. God is the judge, but beastly Babylon destroys.[27] Importantly, the three destructive horses "come," and are not *sent* (Rev. 6:3, 5, 7).[28] Before them comes Christ, who holds the rainbow mark-

---

23. Bauckham, *Theology of the Book of Revelation*, 80.

24. See Bauckham, *Theology of the Book of Revelation*, 80–83; see also Hansen, *Silence and Praise*, 85–103.

25. Hansen, *Silence and Praise*, 67.

26. Hansen, *Silence and Praise*, 117; see also Bauckham, *Theology of the Book of Revelation*, 82.

27. Hansen, *Silence and Praise*, 130.

28. Hansen, *Silence and Praise*, 85.

ing God's covenant with the earth and its inhabitants.[29] He is the one who has overcome at Calvary and shone forth God's covenant faithfulness.[30] When he came to his own, his own did not receive him. They responded with further violence and resistance, as indicated by the three horses who come after him.[31] People continued in their destructive ways instead of repenting (Rev. 9:20–21)—even though repentance is certainly the intended goal of giving them over in judgment (Rev. 11:13).[32] God is seeking the salvation of God's whole creation (5:9; 7:9; 10:11; 11:9; 13:7; 14:6; 17:15), the conversion of the nations.[33] In judgment, all things disfigured by idolatry and the reign of the empire crumble to the ground, that they might be reconstructed according to the ways of God.[34]

Even so, the breaking of the seals and the judgments that come with them are not what sets the world right.[35] These judgments cannot bring rebellious creation in line with God's ways revealed in Christ. Judgments dismantle, but God's justifying work sets things right.[36] It is by the cross that reconciliation is extended and we can enter into life made right. The self-giving, other-nurturing love of the cross matches the result God desires for creation's own self-expression.[37] Since redeemed life means loving expres-

---

29. Hansen, *Silence and Praise*, 86, 88.

30. Hansen, *Silence and Praise*, 88, note 16; see also Romans 3:25—"God displayed [Christ] publicly as the mercy seat (on account of the faithfulness connected with his blood) for proof of the righteousness of God" (author's translation).

31. Hansen, *Silence and Praise*, 89.

32. Hansen, *Silence and Praise*, 89.

33. Hansen, *Silence and Praise*, 122.

34. Hansen, *Silence and Praise*, 2.

35. Bauckham, *Theology of the Book of Revelation*, 83.

36. Hansen, *Silence and Praise*, 67. Justification is rectification.

37. Like Christ, we must "do nothing out of selfish ambition or vain conceit. Rather, in humility value others above yourselves, not looking to your own interests but each of you to the interests of the others. In your relationships with

sion, redemption is not accomplished by means of the judgments. If our new life were extended through dismantling processes, it would be counterproductive to God's purposes for creation's life and inconsistent with the self-sacrificial way God wields power. The resulting dynamic of using judgments to bring the world under God would be a world that cowers under God's will. That type of fear, created by the brutal use of force, is exactly the way the empires of Satan use power.

The seals open on the way to revealing the scroll's message. The message shows how it is that divine power gathers the world under God's rule.[38] Only the slaughtered Lamb is "worthy to take the scroll and to open its seals, because you were slain" (5:9). The reason is that it is a message of bearing crosses. The message of the scroll (the method) is that the ransomed people of God will have to follow after the slaughtered Lamb, the truest demonstration of God's power. "The people of God have been redeemed *from all the nations* (5:9) in order to bear prophetic witness *to all the nations* (11:3–13)."[39] God's will for the redemption of creation happens through the dismantling process of judgments and extending reconciliation through "the sacrificial witness of the elect people who already acknowledge God's rule."[40] This makes God's people more than conquerors—beyond the pattern of conquering (Rom. 8:35–37)—just as Christ was. They will indeed overcome but not as the kingdoms of the world do. "They triumphed over him [Satan] by the

---

one another, have the same mindset as Christ Jesus" (Phil. 2:3–5; see the mindset of Christ in vv. 6–8).

38. Bauckham, *Theology of the Book of Revelation*, 80.

39. Bauckham, *Theology of the Book of Revelation*, 84. "Judgments alone do not lead to repentance (9:20–21). The witness of the witnesses does lead to repentance, though not independently of judgments, but in conjunction with them (11:6, 13)" (Bauckham, 86).

40. Bauckham, *Theology of the Book of Revelation*, 84.

blood of the Lamb and by the word of their testimony; they did not love their lives so much as to shrink from death" (Rev. 12:11).[41] In following the power of God, which lovingly works for the sake of others, they will live *cross*ways to the ways of the empire. Consequently, they may face trouble, hardship, persecution, famine, nakedness, danger, or sword (Rom. 8:35). Yet their faithfulness to the power of God's love revealed in Christ witnesses to the truth of God's reconciling work (see John 17).

The message of the scroll is consistent with the broader New Testament message to the church: "God was reconciling the world to himself in Christ, not counting people's sins against them. And he has committed to us the message of reconciliation. We are therefore Christ's ambassadors, as though God were making his appeal through us. We implore you on Christ's behalf: Be reconciled to God" (2 Cor. 5:19–20). It would be an inaccurate message to the world if it experienced the divine judgments without seeing tangibly in believers the beauty of God's love that works for the sake of others, for the sake of wholeness of life for the world. It would also be an inaccurate message to the world to be able to slaughter faithful Christ followers without any sign that judgments bring, that the empire's own ways guarantee nothing but implosion into death. The message of the scroll is not necessarily one of immediate comfort for Christians. They are called to uncompromised fidelity to Christ, to be ambassadors of reconciliation, which will make them targets for martyrdom (2:13; 20:4). Christians have the honor

---

41. "John insists that the church is a people that has been liberated and forgiven by the blood (death) of the Lamb . . . that it produces faithful and 'victorious' servants who have affirmed their identification with the Lamb's blood by shedding their own blood . . . and that it is destined for ultimate victory and glory, symbolized especially by white robes. . . . Like Jesus himself, the church is symbolized by the colors red and white, slaughtered yet victorious" (Gorman, *Reading Revelation Responsibly*, 130).

of being part of God's method for saving rebels, but loving our neighbors as ourselves—including our enemies—may come at the cost of our own lives. Christians "follow the Lamb wherever he goes" (Rev. 14:4).

Following our leader is difficult, and not just because it may carry heavy costs. Revelation is full of cautions and pleas. The book suggests that some of God's people have themselves been seduced by the lies of the beasts and the harlot. The letters to the seven churches are mixed with praise and blame.[42] The weight of half of the letters falls on the side of warning and challenge, and the letters tend to grow in harshness and intensity as they go on, ending with Laodicea (3:14–21).[43] This revelation is highly concerned for Christians who have become wrapped up in the empire, financially (3:17) or otherwise (2:14, 20). Because God is enthroned, the greater threat to Christians is not any persecution the empire might inflict on them but that Christians will not come out from the empire and will instead be seduced by it.

The Purpose of Revelation

The point of Revelation is to show us the truth of what is going on in the world. Satan is really the one behind the might of the empires we so admire, and we wrongly connect their prosperity with divine blessing. With all of the ways we try to spin their leopard-like bodies, bear claws, and lion's teeth (13:2) as godlike or a sign of divine favor, empires are entirely unlike the slaughtered Lamb of God and the followers of the Holy One.[44] Contrary to the spin,

---

42. Harry O. Maier, *Apocalypse Recalled: the Book of Revelation after Christendom* (Minneapolis: Fortress Press, 2002), 31

43. Maier, *Apocalypse Recalled*, 31–32.

44. The imagery in Revelation about the Roman Empire is a mash-up of imagery from Daniel 7 about four earlier versions of empire: Babylon, Persia,

empires are inherently predators that stay alive by feeding off others, not following the Lamb in loving care for others.[45] They claim to be agents of God, while they actually are sharing Satan's throne. The world is operating under a blanket of lies. The land beast has us falling in step in the delusion.

> The function of propaganda is to make evil look good, the demonic divine, violence like peacemaking, tyranny and oppression like liberation. It makes blind, unquestioning allegiance appear to be freely chosen, religiously appropriate devotion. The grand lie does not appear to start as deception, but only as rhetorical exaggeration. The exaggeration deepens, lengthens, and broadens in an almost organic act of self-distortion. Eventually the rhetoric becomes a blatant falsehood, but now people have not only come to believe the lie, they also live the lie; over time they have been narrated into it. At that point, the exaggeration-turned-falsehood becomes uncontested *and uncontestable* truth, and its effects highly dangerous. Evil in the name of good and of God is now nearly inevitable, as the lie functions as an apocalypse, a religious revelation that only a true Apocalypse can unveil.[46]

The book of Revelation lets us all see the one true God—Father, Son, and Holy Spirit (Rev. 4–5)—and what it means to be people who follow in faithful obedience and witness to his kingdom. Satan's kingdom of the world will give way to

---

Greece, and Alexander's successors. "Roman imperialism brings together all that the previous empires had contained, in terms of geography, power, and bestial corruption" (DeSilva, *Unholy Allegiances*, 43).

45. There is an interesting comparison to the indictments against Egypt in Exodus 1–15 and Rome in Revelation 17–18. See Walter Brueggemann's commentary on Exodus in Vol. 1 of the *New Interpreter's Bible* (Nashville: Abingdon Press, 1994).

46. Gorman, *Reading Revelation Responsibly*, 125ff.

"the kingdom of our Lord and of his Messiah, and he will reign for ever and ever" (Rev. 11:15). Christ's coming reign is such glad tidings to the whole world.

> His kingdom shall cover the whole earth. The Child of Bethlehem shall destroy the works of the devil; every knee shall bow to him and every tongue shall confess him Lord to the glory of God. Oppression and wrong in government, emulation and pride in society, impurity and selfishness in the individual, shall vanish away; righteousness shall fill the earth; the Christmas song shall break into a world chorus; the new Jerusalem shall come down out of heaven; the blight of sin on childhood, womanhood and manhood shall give place to holiness and the joy of liberty. Floating over all seas, ringing among all mountains and echoing through all valleys, shall be heard the Bethlehem cradle song, "Glory to God in the highest, on earth peace, and good will toward [all]," sung by angels and redeemed humanity.[47]

For every person who is faithful to Christ as Lord, we already join in that great chorus.

In Revelation's two-sided narrative, there can be no dual allegiances. We cannot live as good citizens of the empire and our Lord's kingdom. Revelation unveils that there are two different masters behind each of those kingdoms—God and Satan. They are on opposing sides, and the kingdom of this world will give way to God's reign (11:15). We cannot serve both kingdoms (3:14–22); neither God nor Satan allows that.

---

47. J. S. R., "The Power of Christmas," *Nazarene Messenger* 13:26 (December 24, 1908), 12. Our longing for Christ's coming reign focuses our prayers in the Advent season.

Christ's followers must come out of Babylon and its ways (18:4). In the midst of the fray, Christians clear a space for silence (itself an act of resistance) and prayer. They find that God is present and enthroned at the center.[48] In the presence of God in the heavenly throne room, believers join in true praise—not any of the idolatrous praise in which the world is caught up.[49] Even now, having come out of Babylon, rightly ordered life before God pours through their activities, which "brings new creation into expression."[50] Silence clears away for the sake of participation in the glorification of God.[51] Though empires still may try by their methods to stop it, the new life of the world is arriving. The battle was finished on Calvary (Rev. 16:17; see also John 19:30; Col. 2:15).[52]

Heeding Revelation Today

All of this means that Revelation is a timeless message for God's people in every age. Kingdoms rise and fall across history—even though every one of them believes it will never end. The empires of Babylon, Persia, and Greece all fell (Daniel 7). The Roman, Holy Roman, Byzantine, and later empires all fell. We can trust that the empires of today are also not everlasting. Revelation was written during the Roman Empire, guiding Christians toward faithfulness in their circumstances. Yet empires all tend to follow the same characteristics of the Dragon, and lure Christians into the same pitfalls. Christians in every age need to hear the exhortations and promises of Revelation. They need their eyes calibrated so they may faithfully follow God and the Lamb.

---

48. Hansen, *Silence and Praise*, 106, 127.
49. Hansen, *Silence and Praise*, 127.
50. Hansen, *Silence and Praise*, 127.
51. Hansen, *Silence and Praise*, 131.
52. Hansen, *Silence and Praise*, 146.

It would be sad for Christians to ignore Revelation's message about what posture to take with whatever empire is presently at work in the world. We are in danger of doing that if we think it is all a book of clues about end times. To Christians in the thick of their sufferings, we are *assured* that God is unshakably enthroned; the final chapters give *hope* about the ultimate salvation that will come when Christ comes again, makes all things new, and reigns without end. That is deep comfort to those being crushed in the mechanisms of the empire. Otherwise, the messages to the seven first-century churches need to be heeded by all churches at all times, and the eye-opening visions of the book should lead us out of participation in our Babylons and into true worship of God.

EIGHT

Bearing Faithful Witness

They devoted themselves to the apostles' teaching and to fellowship, to the breaking of bread and to prayer.

—*Acts 2:42*

The gifts he gave were that some would be apostles, some prophets, some evangelists, some pastors and teachers, to equip the saints for the work of ministry, for building up the body of Christ, until all of us come to the unity of the faith and of the knowledge of the Son of God, to maturity, to the measure of the full stature of Christ. We must no longer be children, tossed to and fro and blown about by every wind of doctrine, by people's trickery, by their craftiness in deceitful scheming. But speaking the truth in love, we must grow up in every way into him who is the head, into Christ, from whom the whole body, joined and knit together by every ligament with which it is equipped, as each part is working properly, promotes the body's growth in building itself up in love.

—*Ephesians 4:11–16, NRSV*

I urge you, brothers and sisters, to watch out for those who cause divisions and put obstacles in your way that are contrary to the teaching you have learned. Keep away from them.

—*Romans 16:17*

Guided by the Apostles

The apostles handed on what they received from the Lord (1 John 1:1–5). Their firsthand accounts of Christ became the basis for the New Testament and the parameter for how the church read the Scriptures and understood the Christian faith (Luke 24:27, 45; Acts 8:30–35; 2 Thess. 2:15; 3:6; 2 Tim. 1:13; 3:10–17). The apostles, those whom they taught, and the generations to follow were zealous to remain faithful to the revelation of God in Christ Jesus. There were claims being made—even in Christianity's infancy—that did not fit the testimony of the eyewitnesses; several New Testament letters name these false teachings and/or teachers. Some people questioned the apostles' teaching about the resurrection of the dead (1 Cor. 15:12; see also Acts 4:2). Others suggested the day of the Lord had already come (2 Thess. 2:2), as if we could miss the proclamation (1 Thess. 4:16) or "the splendor of his coming" (2 Thess. 2:8).

In the centuries to follow, Christianity continued to fend off divergent teachings about resurrection and God's work of new creation. These were hard teachings to embrace in the Greco-Roman world because they were so accustomed to thinking about escaping bodily existence, which they considered to be bad or inferior.[1] The Judeo-Christian teachings about the goodness of creation, God's covenant with it, God's faithfulness to save it from the grip of sin and death, and the final hope of transforming it for eternity were so backward to the direction of people's escapist thinking. It was more than their cultural sensibilities could stomach for Christianity to teach that the Son of God be-

---

1. For example, Justin Martyr (AD 100–165) wrote to explain Christianity's doctrine of the resurrection to a wider Greco-Roman audience who would have thought resurrection was undesirable (see "On the Resurrection," especially Chapters 2–5, 7–10, http://www.ccel.org/ccel/schaff/anf01.viii.viii.ii.html).

came incarnate in human flesh (fully human) and that his body was resurrected for eternal life (as the firstfruits of all who die in the Lord).

No matter how diligent the apostles and those who followed were in laying down what they received and protecting it from corruption, they were always working in the midst of countercurrents. Some of those were existing currents within Judaism (Acts 4:2); some were the alluring currents of sin and death at work in the world; and others were the currents of the broader Greco-Roman worldview. In the history of Christianity countercurrents have always gained toeholds among believers. Nevertheless, we still have the compass of Scripture and the guideline of the apostolic witness for reading it.[2] That apostolic guidance was the rule by which scriptures were faithfully interpreted. As Augustine cautioned, "Hasty and careless readers are led astray by many and manifold obscurities and ambiguities, substituting one meaning for another; and in some places they cannot hit upon even a fair interpretation."[3] Without apostolic guidance, there could be as many different ways to read passages as there are readers.[4] Augustine not only taught his congregation the rule of apostolic interpretation

---

2. Augustine (AD 354–430) calls the legacy of the apostles the "rules for the interpretation of Scripture" (*On Christian Teaching*, Preface §1, http://faculty.georgetown.edu/jod/augustine/ddc1.html). It is critical to Augustine to lay out the apostolic rules: "the man who lays down rules for interpretation is like one who teaches reading, that is, shows others how to read for themselves. So that, just as he who knows how to read is not dependent on some one else, when he finds a book, to tell him what is written in it, so the man who is in possession of the rules which I here attempt to lay down, if he meet with an obscure passage in the books which he reads, will not need an interpreter to lay open the secret to him, but, holding fast by certain rules, and following up certain indications, will arrive at the hidden sense without any error, or at least without falling into any gross absurdity" (Preface §9).

3. Augustine, *On Christian Teaching*, 2.6.7.

4. Vincent of Lérins, *A Commonitory*, chapter 2, paragraph 5, http://www.ccel.org/ccel/schaff/npnf211.iii.iii.html.

but also about figurative language,[5] idioms,[6] ambiguities,[7] difficulties of translation,[8] and other hindrances to reading the Scriptures soundly. He taught them sound doctrine and biblical interpretation skills.

This book has been an exercise in reading the Scriptures according to the apostolic rule of faith as summarized in the Nicene Creed. As the vastly spread-out church gathered in AD 325 and 381, they found agreement on what counted as a faithful reading of the Scriptures, according to the teaching of the apostles each congregation had maintained (a common, apostolic, and orthodox reading).[9] They summarized the Bible's teaching on eschatology with these phrases: Christ "will come again in glory to judge the living and the dead, and his kingdom will have no end," and "we look for the resurrection of the dead, and the life of the world to come." Any other way of reading Scripture is not the Christian faith as the apostles received it and passed it on and does not follow the rule of Christian orthodoxy.

The Problem of Dispensationalism

Tragically we find ourselves in a period in Christian history where a nineteenth-century countercurrent has gotten

---

5. Augustine, *On Christian Teaching*, 2.10.15.

6. Augustine, *On Christian Teaching*, 2.14.21.

7. Augustine, *On Christian Teaching*, 2.12.17.

8. Augustine, *On Christian Teaching*, 2.11.16.

9. These three criteria can be seen in how the church picked which books to include in the New Testament (see the Muratorian Fragment from the second century AD, http://www.earlychristianwritings.com/muratorian.html). They are also the criteria used by the church in how to read the Scriptures (see St. Vincent of Lerins, *Commonitorium*, 2.5–6 from the fifth century AD, http://www.ccel. org/ccel/schaff/npnf211.iii.iii.html). Tertullian (AD 160–220) offers an account of how the early church handed on the witness of the apostles (see *Prescription Against Heretics*, chapters 20–22, 28, 37–38, http://www.newadvent.org/fathers /0311.htm). For Augustine's instructions on how to read Scripture, see *On Christian Teaching*, especially the preface and Book II.4–14, http://faculty.georgetown. edu/jod/augustine/ddc1.html.

a firm toehold among American Evangelicals. The birth and growth of this countercurrent is well documented.[10] In the 1830s, John Nelson Darby developed a new way of interpreting Scripture known today as premillennial dispensationalism (or dispensational premillennialism). New in the history of Christianity, Darby started teaching about rapture instead of resurrection,[11] a two-stage future coming of Christ,[12] and history being broken up into separate dispensations for the church. He brought his controversial ideas from Scotland to the United States during several visits between 1859 and 1877. The seeds of his campaigns did not fully germinate until the Scofield Reference Bible (first released in 1909) again published Darby's dispensationalist teachings in a second edition on the heels of World War I (1917). Audiences were looking for any way to make meaning of the senseless magnitude of the war's devastation. Dispensationalism's grim picture of world destruction and escape for believers seemed

10. See, for example, Barbara R. Rossing, *The Rapture Exposed: The Message of Hope in the Book of Revelation*, especially her first three chapters: "The Destructive Racket of Rapture," "The Invention of the Rapture," and "The Rapture Script for the Middle East." Even those without access to her book can find helpful historical accounts online: for example, Timothy Weber, "Dispensational Premillennialism: The Dispensationalist Era," *Christian History Institute* 61 (1999), https://christianhistoryinstitute.org/magazine/article/dispensational-premillennialism-the-dispensationalist-era/. Readers can also conduct web searches for terms such as "John Nelson Darby," "Premillennial Dispensationalism," and "Scofield Bible" in order to find the history and development of this modern countercurrent. The Christian History Institute also offers thematic issues (nos. 61, 70, 100, 112) on relevant topics for readers to see how some of the themes in this book unfolded after the New Testament period: https://christianhistoryinstitute.org/magazine/issues.

11. The idea was first based on misreading 1 Thess. 4:17 (see an explanation of this text in chapter 6). The assumption about rapture has created the misreading of Matt. 24:39–42 (see my explanation in chapter 4 that being taken is a bad thing in the Bible); and John 14:1–3 is also misread (see my explanation in chapter 6 about the double stitch of us having a dwelling place in the Father that is followed by the Father and Son coming to dwell in us in v. 23).

12. Rossing, *The Rapture Exposed*, 22.

fitting because it provided a way for people to understand the war and regain their bearings.

Cyrus I. Scofield's Bible sold millions of copies and "became the version of the Bible through which Americans read their scriptures throughout much of the twentieth century. Scofield's notes and headings were woven in with the biblical text itself, elevating dispensationalism to a level of biblical authority."[13] Since 1917, American authors have recast the prophetic web of dispensationalism to fit each American crisis of the twentieth century—whether it was with Germany in World War II or the Soviet Union in the Cold War. Hal Lindsey, Tim LaHaye, John Hagee, and others have made decades-long careers of continually re-mapping dispensationalism onto the shifting landscape of American events. One effect has been a century of shaping American Evangelical imagination to see the movement of God, the message of the Bible, and the history of creation all culminating ultimately in the affairs of the United States and this exact moment in history. Without being aware of it, Americans have been conditioned to see themselves and their country as the linchpin of the world and history—all immersed in religious significance through a continually readjusted "Christian" mythology.[14] When one doomsday prediction fails, new calculations are released. When one of America's enemies fails to be *the* Enemy their reading of Scripture demands, they match up another American enemy with biblical passages. Many Evangelicals have un-

---

13. Rossing, *The Rapture Exposed*, 23.

14. It is sobering that this mythologizing of America's affairs within God's providence is a similar practice to what Rome did in its time. Revelation exposed Rome as an agent of Satan (not of the divine); Rome operated in self-interest and profited off the advantage it had over others. The United States is no less the biggest empire of this day as Rome was of its day. Perhaps Christians in America need a new book of Revelation to see the predatory claws of the beast and the lure of the harlot contrasted against the call to follow the Lamb.

knowingly been immersed in a theology and a way to read Scripture that is a nineteenth-century invention—a countercurrent to the commonly held, orthodox Christianity of the apostles.

In dispensationalism, the rapture of believers and the obliteration of the world each contradict "the resurrection of the dead and the life of the world to come." These are not just contradictory events taught about the end of history. They make fundamentally different claims about God and God's intentions for creation. Rather than God being jealous for and faithful to the world—from the beginning on into eternity—the world and our bodies are discarded. They end in destruction instead of completion in the glory of God. God and believers abandon ship. "Salvation" and "the Gospel" are turned into spiritual escape instead of earth receiving her King. Sin and death get the final word in claiming the world over our Alpha and Omega. This kind of theology teaches that God ends the world but is not the world's End. Whatever eternity we have is thought to be an entirely different creation than this one—a second creation, instead of all things being made new in the love of God. Given what we have explored in the Scriptures and what Jesus's disciples handed on to the church, it is not possible to reconcile dispensationalist doctrine with Christian doctrine confessed through the centuries. Many believers stand at a crossroad as significant as choosing between the commonly held, orthodox Christianity of the apostles and the countercurrent birthed by John Nelson Darby.

The Problem of Fabricated Signs

The detailed predictions made by dispensationalist leaders *sound* technical, complex, and scholarly. The exactness of the predictions offers certainty in uncertain times or the illusion of control when circumstances feel out of control. Dispensationalism promises a mechanism for steering our destiny. Mastery of the details can become a place of refuge when nothing else in the world is making sense. We can also feel significant—we are playing an important insider role—when so many personal or global factors marginalize us.[15] However, dispensationalism is a fabricated theory based on its own invented rules for interpretation—for instance, that somehow the seventy weeks mentioned in Daniel 9:25–27 are the framework for "God's whole biblical plan for the end times."[16] Dispensationalists' rule of interpretation for Daniel 9:25–27 is that each week actually represents seven years; the sequence of 490 years can be paused and restarted; we have been on pause at the end of week sixty-nine since Christ's crucifixion—and this added two-thousand-year gap gives space for the church in the seventy weeks. That is a lot to make of three verses that do not say any of these things but are, instead, a reference to 168 BC, "when the tyrannical emperor Antiochus Epiphanes desecrated the Jewish temple and set up a statue of the Greek god Zeus."[17]

Fabricating gaps within biblical texts is a common practice for dispensationalists. John Hagee, for instance, inserts a gap of thousands of years in Isaiah 9:6, between the announcement of the child being born and the second half of the verse, saying "the government shall be upon his shoulders."[18] These complicated webs created by giving new meanings to certain prophecies and fabricating gaps that do not

---

15. See David Ludden, "Why Do People Believe in Conspiracy Theories? The Need to Find Order in a Confusing World," *Psychology Today* (January 6, 2018), https://www.psychologytoday.com/us/blog/talking-apes/201801/why-do -people-believe-in-conspiracy-theories.

16. Rossing, *The Rapture Exposed*, 25.

17. Rossing, *The Rapture Exposed*, 26.

18. Rossing, *The Rapture Exposed*, 28.

exist in the Bible help dispensationalists map and remap their story onto selected portions of Western history.[19]

In the second century AD, Irenaeus offered an analogy of what the heretics were doing in his day: they were taking the mosaic of Scripture and apostolic teaching and turning the variously colored tiles into a different mosaic, according to their own, independently derived rule of interpretation.[20] Anyone can change around the tiles of the mosaic according to the rule they follow—for example, turn the image of a king into the image of "a dog or a fox."[21] However, Irenaeus stressed that the truthful rule, giving what the mosaic actually is, is faithfully preserved in the apostolic teaching of the church.[22] Dispensationalism's rule does not pass that test; it is independently derived from the 1830s onward.

Another caution is that dispensationalists' prophetic work is not entirely unlike what astrologers were doing in Augustine's time. Astrologers' predictions, based on the movement of lights in the sky, essentially "have their origin in certain signs of things being arbitrarily fixed upon by the presumption of men."[23] In other words, they selectively chose what lights to note and what meaning to give those lights based on their beliefs. But "it was not because [the lights] had meaning that they were attended to, but it

---

19. Rossing, *The Rapture Exposed*, 25.

20. Irenaeus, *Against Heresies*, 1.8.1.

21. Richard A. Norris, "Theology and Language in Irenaeus of Lyon," in *Recent Studies in Early Christianity: a Collection of Scholarly Essays*, ed. by Everett Ferguson (New York: Garland Publishing, Inc., 1999), 187.

22. Norris, "Theology and Language in Irenaeus," 189.

23. Augustine, *On Christian Teaching*, 2.22.34. He warns: "As, then, from the stars which God created and ordained, men have drawn lying omens of their own fancy, so also from things that are born, or in any other way come into existence under the government of God's providence, if there chance only to be something unusual in the occurrence—as when a mule brings forth young, or an object is struck by lightning—men have frequently drawn omens by conjectures of their own, and have committed them to writing, as if they had drawn them by rule" (2.23.36).

was by attending to and marking them that they came to have meaning. And so they are made different for different people, according to their several notions and prejudices."[24] This is a similar concern to what Irenaeus had with making tiles into an image of one's own choosing.

Concerning people who try to divine "things in the past and future," Augustine says that God gives them over to the folly of their desires: "many things turn out agreeably to their observances, and ensnared by these successes, they become more eagerly inquisitive, and involve themselves further and further in a labyrinth of most pernicious error."[25] Christians should not be looking to "interpret signs," whether they are picked out from among celestial, geological, and historical events, or from the Bible itself. That way of operating is a new form of divination dressed up in Christian clothing. Augustine clarified that astrological observations certainly should not be factored into our interpretation of Scripture.[26] However, the forbidden practice of making meaning out of events in the sky is being done under the banner of dispensationalism[27]—just as world events are also being factored into their prophetic web. Yet how can any teacher claim to know or figure out

---

24. Augustine, *On Christian Teaching*, 2.24.37.

25. Augustine, *On Christian Teaching*, 2.23.35.

26. Here is what Augustine says about paying attention to the movement of heavenly bodies: "And this knowledge, although in itself it involves no superstition, renders very little, indeed almost no assistance, in the interpretation of Holy Scripture, and by engaging the attention unprofitably is a hindrance rather; and as it is closely related to the very pernicious error of the diviners of the fates, it is more convenient and becoming to neglect it" (*On Christian Teaching*, 2.29.46).

27. John Hagee's *Four Blood Moons* (Worthy Publishing, 2013) is a prime example. One helpful critique of Hagee's book can be found in the sermon by Greg Boyd referenced in a previous chapter, "The End of the World as You Know It" (although the whole sermon breaks down "signs theology," his critique of Hagee's book starts at 37:25: https://whchurch.org/sermon/the-end-of-the-world-as-you-know-it/).

when Christ will return, when even the Son of God does not have that? "But about that day or hour no one knows, not even the angels in heaven, nor the Son, but only the Father" (Matt. 24:36; see also Mark 13:32). Every prediction made about Christ's return has been wrong.[28]

Many dispensationalists are looking to the horizon for signs that Christ and his reign are coming—and, with it, some type of cataclysmic battle. On one hand, this is strange given the proclamation of the gospel in Christ's ministry that the kingdom of God is already at hand (Mark 1:15). The last days started in Christ, his kingdom has been inaugurated, and it has been going on for quite some time now. Jesus taught that participation in eternal life began for anyone who heard his voice and followed (John 3:36; 5:24; 6:47, 54); they had already crossed into that eternal life of knowing "the only true God, and Jesus Christ" (17:3). Life under God's lordship begins in baptism as we are united with Christ in his death and raised to new life (Rom. 6:4). Believers no longer belong to the darkness, kingdoms, or powers at work in the world, but to their Lord. In and through Christ we have "overcome the evil one" (1 John 2:13–14; see 4:4; 5:4).

On the other hand, it is precisely in Christ's crucifixion, death, and resurrection that the battle of all battles was fought and won; "having disarmed the powers and authorities, he made a public spectacle of them, triumphing

---

28. Many articles are available that document failed attempts to predict Christ's return: William Miller predicted 1844, https://en.wikipedia.org/wiki/Great_Disappointment; Hal Lindsey predicted 1988, https://americanvision.org/1753/hal-lindsey-making-predictionsagain/; Tim LaHaye predicted in the lifetime of those born in 1914, https://www.premierchristianity.com/Blog/It-s-time-to-leave-Tim-LaHaye-s-Rapture-theology-behind. *Christian History* devoted issue 61 (1999) to highlighting ways the end has been handled across the centuries, with several articles giving attention to dispensational premillenialism, https://www.christianitytoday.com/history/issues/issue-61/.

Believers are not given the task of divining signs and timetables. We are called to faithfulness to our Lord.

over them by the cross" (Col. 2:15). Truly, "it is finished" (John 19:30; see also 16:33). The only blood spilled to win this "battle" was his own (Rev. 5:9; 7:14; 12:10–12; 19:13). Believers may also be killed for siding with the triumphant Christ, but we are not accomplishing more than what Christ has already done (6:10; 14:20; 16:6; 17:6; 18:24; 19:2); we are remaining in the power of the cross and resurrection. Given Christ's faithfulness, "God exalted him to the highest place and gave him the name that is above every name, that at the name of Jesus every knee should bow, in heaven and on earth and under the earth, and every tongue acknowledge that Jesus Christ is Lord, to the glory of God the Father" (Phil. 2:9–11). The Lamb of God "has triumphed" (Rev. 5:5); he "is Lord of lords and King of kings" (17:14); he holds "the keys of death and Hades" (1:18). To bring the end of all history and wickedness in the world, it will only take a word from the Lord—the double-edged sword from Christ's mouth. The coming of Christ—the Way, the Truth, the Life—will expose and dispel every falsehood infecting the world (see Heb. 4:12–13; Rev. 1:16; 19:15).

Believers are not given the task of divining signs and timetables. We are called to faithfulness to our Lord—who suffered crucifixion and death for the sake of his enemies. He was lifted up to draw all people to himself (John 12:32). In God's great love for the world, God desires that the world would repent and come into the light. God is seeking and providing for the conversion of the world in Christ. At the same time, the world will face the consequences of being unrepentant, unless it turns to following the Lamb. Believers, thus, "follow the Lamb wherever he goes" (Rev. 14:4). They suffer on account of Christ—but not for the sake of suffering. It is for the sake of love for their enemies—that they might turn and have life in Christ. "We are therefore Christ's ambassadors, as though God were making his appeal through us. We implore you on Christ's behalf: Be reconciled to God" (2 Cor. 5:20). In spite of any suffering or death they endure, Christians live in Christ's victory over Satan and worldly powers: "They triumphed over him by the blood of the Lamb and by the word of their testimony" (Rev. 12:11; see also 17:14). Those who follow the empires of the world (Satan's beast) are simply drinking the adulteries of those empires (14:8) and, in turn, drinking God's judgment upon themselves (14:10; 16:6). We long for Christ to return, to put a final end to the destructiveness of sin and death in the world, and to set all things right. But right now God is graciously holding open the door for repentance. So we remain faithful workers in the field. We are not set to the task of divining signs and predicting the future. We know that God is enthroned, that Christ has won, and that we are unshakably in God's care—whether in life or death. Believers do "not love their lives so much as to shrink from death" (12:11). We live the life of love to which we are called as faithful witnesses (John 15:9–26). That life is not until we somehow escape this world. That life is our destiny in the love of the Father, Son, and Holy Spirit. It is our present participation in the coming life of the world.

The end for the world is not a mysteriously preordained sequence of events for us to correctly identify or navigate. God is the End for the world. God's gift for the world from the beginning, as our Beginning, is that we would abide in and live out of the love of the Father, Son, and Holy Spirit. We are not living in a world meant to progress according to a predetermined sovereign plan. We are not trying to arrange all pieces of the world to be frozen into the perfect family photograph God has preordained. We are living in a world meant to explore fellowship in love for God and neighbor. There are things that will happen *at* Christ's return in order to bring creation into the fullness of eternal divine life. That does not mean there is a breadcrumb trail to lead us to the moment of Christ's return or that Christ's return will be a long, drawn-out process we have to navigate. We entrust ourselves into God's care, for God to do the work of new creation that we cannot do for ourselves.

The Eschatological Task of Believers

Our Christian theology and devotion are connected with what we do in the world. Our eschatology is no different. Here are a few examples of how it is connected to our life as believers.

First, God is committed to the world and its well-being. Christians should be committed to it as well. Humans were formed out of the earth to pour themselves into the nurture and care of the earth and its creatures. We were not created for self-interest. We are of the earth and for the earth. As the Law was laid out before Israel (Genesis through Deuteronomy), much of it paves life-giving pathways for how to farm, treat animals, and observe the rhythms of time. All of this points to the life of the world that finds its fulfillment in Christ, now and forever (Col. 1:15–20). The church should be leading the charge to protect the environment against degrading practices and economic exploitation—any form of human self-interest or expediency. The church is bearing witness to relationships that are eternal, for the life of the world to come. People of the coming age should be grieved by the injustices against the environment, the groaning of the earth, and threats to entire species. We should be doers of justice, practicing right relationships. One area to start is with regulating our consumption. We can decrease our environmental footprint by minimizing our consumption, making sure what we consume is sustainably and responsibly produced, advocating on behalf of creation, and being agents of restoration.

Second, we should pay attention to our bodies. God cares for our bodies, giving us daily, weekly, and seasonal cycles of work and rest. There is sacredness to all time in the sanctuary of God's creation. Keeping rhythms of time in our lives is to participate in and bear witness to the abundance of life God is gifting to the world.[29] We can sleep when it is nighttime and keep the Sabbath as an act of glorifying God and delighting in God's gift of good life. We do not do it to be legalistic but to savor the gift. We also recognize that not all things are yet as they will be and that we may need to respond to immediate crises of our neighbors in rest times; but we do not order our lives in disregard to life-giving, God-glorifying rhythms.

Along with keeping godly rhythms of time, we should also affirm the goodness of our creaturely physicality by tending to our health. Jesus fed hungry crowds and made sick people well. God has given us a world of flavorful, nutrient-rich foods. We should not deny the goodness of the world and our bodies through starving ourselves (except for the purpose of prayerful fasting). We also should not misdirect our love toward food by pursuing or eating it as an end in itself; food should not become the master we serve or a base necessity of life. Rather, we delight in it as a gift from the Lord, in fellowship with God and neighbor, unto the glorification of the Lord.[30] We practice holy eating. We also practice loving care for our bodies and the bodies of others through proper hygiene, diet, sleep, movement, healthcare,

29. See Alexander Schmemann, "The Time of Mission," in *For the Life of the World* (Crestwood, NY: St. Vladimir's Seminary Press, 1963), 47–65.

30. See the Wesley mealtime prayer, "Grace before Meat" (quoted by Michael E. Lodahl and April Cordero Maskiewicz in *Renewal in Love: Living Holy Lives in God's Good Creation* [Kansas City, MO: Beacon Hill Press of Kansas City, 2014], 94, 96).

socialization, reflection, and more. We are holistic in loving our neighbor as ourselves.

God has not made us to be slaves to work, food, possessions, or pleasure. Humankind is meant to image God in the world in being creatures who love our neighbors as ourselves. We do that in every facet of our physicality both now and in our resurrection life. Thus, we are *thirdly* more than brute animals in our sexuality. We are imagers of God. How we have or do not have sex is about who God is, and consequently, who we are as God's creation (see 1 Cor. 7).[31] Sex and sexuality are a good part of God's creation (Gen. 1:28; 2:24–25), and are another dimension of our personhood through which we can glorify God. Paul taught the Corinthians to "flee from sexual immorality. All other sins a person commits are outside the body, but whoever sins sexually, sins against their own body. Do you not know that your bodies are temples of the Holy Spirit, who is in you, whom you have received from God? You are not your own; you were bought at a price. Therefore honor God with your bodies" (1 Cor. 6:18–20). We are not an inner self or soul that is going to escape from physicality. We are earthlings created to shine God's love.

The Son of God has become truly human to recreate us in true humanity, over which sin and death have no hold—a humanity of the coming age. "Whatever happens," says Paul, "conduct yourselves in a manner worthy of the gospel of Christ" (Phil. 1:27; see also 2 Cor. 1:12; 1 Tim. 3:15). We are neither to despise our bodies nor love them too much but, in all things, delight in the richness of God's good creation in glorification of God. We are neither to be consumed nor consume others. In not having sex outside of

---

31. This is Beth Felker Jones's message. She unpacks this point wonderfully in *Faithful: A Theology of Sex* (Grand Rapids: Zondervan, 2015).

the covenant bond of marriage or in how married couples have sex, both are ways of expressing other-nurturing love and giving ourselves in shared life with fellow creatures in thanks and praise to God. No facet of life, no time, and no place in all creation is to be lived outside of God's self-giving, other-nurturing love. All creaturely life is sacred: from, in, and unto the glory of the Lord.

Conclusion

As was promised in the introductory chapter, this book has not offered a roadmap of end-times events that would help us predict the end of time. Instead we have looked at God's intentions from the dawn of time to bless creation with the glory of God's presence and the ways God has faithfully persevered on behalf of God's sanctuary-creation. Christ gained supremacy on Calvary by filling all things and holding all things together in the glory of God's love—thus, reconciling to God "all things, whether things on earth or things in heaven, by making peace through his blood, shed on the cross" (Col. 1:20; see 2:9–10). Every other power at work in the world was disarmed, exposed, and made subject under Christ (Col. 2:15; Rev. 12:10-12). Now is the time to repent; the kingdom of God is begun. The return of Christ the King will bring an end to wickedness; everyone who "does not believe stands condemned already because they have not believed in the name of God's one and only Son. This is the verdict: Light has come into the world, but people loved darkness instead of light because their deeds were evil" (John 3:18–19). All provisional judgments against evildoers (meant to spur repentance) will end with final judgment. With the casting away of any remnant powers and their devotees, along with the full coming of God's glory, everlasting life will come to creation—the dead will be raised, all bodies will be transformed, the heavens and the earth will be made new. We do not have to wait for this eternal life in God's glory. We can participate in it now, in a provisional way.

Christians today are being flooded with teachings that do not follow the commonly held, orthodox Christianity handed down from the apostles. One objective of this book has been to read the Scriptures in a way that is faithful to the way Christ's disciples taught the church to read them. It may sound foreign to some readers and be a challenge to adjust to it. However, as our imaginations are calibrated to read and think according to the confession of the Christian faith, believers will find great hope and comfort in the faith. With that, we may also join in singing "Joy to the World" with new excitement for the second advent of Christ.

> *Joy to the world; The Lord is come;*
> *Let Earth receive her King:*
> *Let every heart prepare him room,*
> *And heaven and nature sing.*

> *Joy to the earth, The Saviour reigns;*
> *Let us our songs employ;*
> *While fields and floods, rocks, hills, and plains*
> *Repeat the sounding joy.*

> *No more let sins and sorrows grow,*
> *Nor thorns infest the ground:*
> *He comes to make his blessings flow*
> *Far as the curse is found.*

> *He rules the world with truth and grace,*
> *And makes the nations prove*
> *The glories of his righteousness,*
> *And wonders of his love.*

After John saw the transformed life of the heavens and the earth, in Revelation 22:20, he recorded hearing: "He who testifies to these things says, 'Yes, I am coming soon.'" I hope our response is the same as John's: *"Amen. Come, Lord Jesus."*

Bibliography

Works Cited

Augustine, *On Christian Doctrine*. https://faculty.georgetown.edu
/jod/augustine/ddc1.html.

Bauckham, Richard. "Descent to the Underworld," 154-156. *The Anchor Bible Dictionary*, Vol. 2. New York: Doubleday, 1992.

———. "The Holiness of Jesus and His Disciples in the Gospel of John," 95–113. In *Holiness and Ecclesiology in the New Testament*. Ed. by Kent E. Brower and Andy Johnson. Grand Rapids: William B. Eerdmans Publishing Company, 2007.

———. *The Theology of the Book of Revelation*. Cambridge: Cambridge University Press, 1993.

Bell, Rob. *Love Wins: A Book about Heaven, Hell, and the Fate of Every Person Who Ever Lived*. New York: HarperOne, 2011.

Boyd, Greg. *Rescuing Revelation: Sermon Series*. https://whchurch.org
/sermon_series/rescuing-revelation/.

———. "The End of the World as You Know It." *Rescuing Revelation: Sermon Series*. https://www.youtube.com/watch?v
=HoWHzuYF798.

Brown, William P. *Structure, Role, and Ideology in the Hebrew and Greek Texts of Genesis 1:1–2:3*. Atlanta: Scholars Press, 1993.

———. *The Seven Pillars of Creation: The Bible, Science, and the Ecology of Wonder*. New York: Oxford University Press, 2010.

Brueggemann, Walter. "Exodus." In *The New Interpreter's Bible*, Vol. 1. Nashville: Abingdon Press, 1994.

Charlesworth, James H., ed. "1 Enoch." In *The Old Testament Pseudepigrapha*. Peabody, MA: Hendrickson Publishers, 2010.

Christian History Institute, The. https://christianhistoryinstitute.org
/magazine/issues.

Cotter, David W. *Genesis: Berit Olam, Studies in Hebrew Narrative & Poetry*. Collegeville, MN: Liturgical Press, 2003.

Crockett, William, ed. *Four Views on Hell*. Grand Rapids: Zondervan, 1992.

Culpepper, R. Alan. "The Gospel of Luke," 1-490. *The New Interpreter's Bible*, Vol. IX. Nashville: Abingdon Press, 1995.

Dabney, D. Lyle. "The Nature of the Spirit: Creation as a Premonition of God," 71–86. In *The Work of the Spirit: Pneumatology and Pentecostalism*. Edited by Michael Welker. Grand Rapids: Eerdmans, 2006.

Davids, Peter H. *The Epistle of James*. The New International Greek Testament Commentary. Grand Rapids: Eerdmans, 1982.

DeSilva, David A. *Unholy Allegiances: Heeding Revelation's Warning*. Peabody, MA: Hendrickson Publishers, 2013.

Duke, Rodney K. "Eternal Torment or Destruction? Interpreting Final Judgment Texts." *Evangelical Quarterly* 88.3 (2016/17): 237-258.

Ellens, J. Harold. "Afterlife and Underworld in the Bible," 1–5. In *Heaven, Hell and the Afterlife: Eternity in Judaism, Christianity, and Islam*, Volume 1: End Time and Afterlife in Judaism. Ed. by J. Harold Ellens. Santa Barbara: Praeger, 2013.

Enns, Paul. *Heaven Revealed*. Chicago: Moody Publishers, 2011.

Fretheim, Terrence. "The Book of Genesis." In *The New Interpreter's Bible*, Vol. 1. Nashville: Abingdon Press, 1994.

Fudge, Edward William, and Robert A. Peterson. *Two Views of Hell: A Biblical & Theological Dialogue*. Downers Grove, IL: InterVarsity Press, 2000.

Gorman, Michael J. *Reading Revelation Responsibly: Uncivil Worship and Witness: Following the Lamb into the New Creation*. Eugene, OR: Cascade Books, 2011.

Gowan, Donald E. *Eschatology in the Old Testament*. Philadelphia: Fortress Press, 1986.

Green, John, and Hank Green. "Noah's Ark and Floods in the Ancient Near East: Crash Course World Mythology #16." Crash Course: https://youtu.be/VA3j5_vKQfc.

Greib, Katherine. *The Story of Romans: A Narrative Defense of God's Righteousness*. Louisville, KY: Westminster John Knox Press, 2002.

Gulley, Norman R. "Death, New Testament." In *Anchor Bible Dictionary*: *Vol. 2*. New York: Doubleday, 1992.

Hagee, John. *Four Blood Moons*. Brentwood, TN: Worthy Publishing, 2013.

Hamilton, Victor P. *The Book of Genesis: Chapters 1-17*. New International Commentary on the Old Testament. Grand Rapids: William B. Eerdmans Publishing Company, 1990.

Hansen, Ryan L. *Silence and Praise: Rhetorical Cosmology and Political Theology in the Book of Revelation*. Minneapolis: Fortress Press, 2014.

Helsel, Philip Samuel Browning. "Hades, Hell, and Sheol: The Reception History of the King James Version in American Fundamentalism." In *Heaven, Hell, and the Afterlife: Eternity in Judaism, Christianity, and Islam*, Vol. 2: *End Time and Afterlife in Christianity*. Ed. by J. Harold Ellens. Santa Barbara: Praeger, 2013.

Hess, Richard S., and David Toshio Tsumura, eds. *I Studied Inscriptions from before the Flood: Ancient Near Eastern, Literary, and Linguistic Approaches to Genesis 1–11. Sources for Biblical and Theological Study*, Vol. 4. Winona Lake, IN: Eisenbrauns, 1994.

Hill, F. E. "The Beauty of Holiness." *The Nazarene Messenger* 3:30 (December 21, 1899): 7.

Irenaeus of Lyons, *Against Heresies*. In *The Apostolic Fathers with Justin Martyr and Irenaeus*. Ante-Nicene Fathers, Vol. 1. Edinburgh: T&T Clark; Grand Rapids: Eerdmans, 1885. https://www.ccel.org/ccel/schaff/anf01.html.

———, *The Demonstration of the Apostolic Preaching*. Translated by Armitage Robinson. New York: The Macmillan Co., 1920. https://www.ccel.org/ccel/irenaeus/demonstr.iv.html.

Johnson, Andy. "Firstfruits and Death's Defeat: Metaphor in Paul's Rhetorical Strategy in 1 Cor 15:20-28." *Word & World* 16.4 (1996): 456-464.

———. "On Removing a Trump Card: Flesh and Blood and the Reign of God." *Bulletin for Biblical Research* 13.2 (2003): 175–192.

———. "Our God Reigns: The Body of the Risen Lord in Luke 24." *Word & World* 22.2 (2002), 133–43.

———. "Resurrection, Ascension and the Developing Portrait of the God of Israel in Acts." *Scottish Journal of Theology* 57.2 (2004), 146–62.

———. "Ripples of the Resurrection in the Triune Life of God: Reading Luke 24 with Eschatological and Trinitarian Eyes." *Horizons in Biblical Theology* 24.2 (2002), 87–110.

———. "The 'New Creation,' the Crucified and Risen Christ, and the Temple: A Pauline Audience for Mark." *Journal of Theological Interpretation* 1.2 (2007): 171–91.

———. "Turning the World Upside Down in 1 Corinthians 15: Apocalyptic Epistemology, the Resurrected Body, and the New Creation." *The Evangelical Quarterly* 75.4 (2003): 291–309.

Johnston, Philip S., "Gehenna." In *New Interpreter's Dictionary of the Bible D–H*, Vol. 2. Nashville: Abingdon Press, 2007.

Jones, Beth Felker. *Faithful: A Theology of Sex*. Grand Rapids: Zondervan, 2015.

Justin Martyr. *On the Resurrection*. In *The Apostolic Fathers with Justin Martyr and Irenaeus*. Ante-Nicene Fathers, Vol. 1. Edinburgh: T&T Clark; Grand Rapids: Eerdmans, 1885. https://www.ccel.org/ccel/schaff/anf01.html.

Kaiser, Walter C. *Preaching and Teaching the Last Things: Old Testament Eschatology for the Life of the Church*. Grand Rapids: Baker Academic, 2011.

Kvanvig, Jonathan L. *The Problem of Hell*. New York: Oxford University Press, 1993.

Lam, Joseph. "Biblical Creation in its Ancient Near Eastern Context." *BioLogos* (April 21, 2010), http://biologos.org/uploads/projects/lam_scholarly_essay.pdf.

Lodahl, Michael. *Claiming Abraham: Reading the Bible and the Qur'an Side by Side*. Grand Rapids: Brazos Press, 2010.

Lodahl, Michael, and April Cordero Maskiewicz. *Renewal in Love: Living Holy Lives in God's Good Creation*. Kansas City, MO: Beacon Hill Press of Kansas City, 2014.

Lorey, Frank. "The Flood of Noah and the Flood of Gilgamesh." *Institute for Creation Research* (1997): https://www.icr.org/article/414/.

Ludden, David. "Why Do People Believe in Conspiracy Theories? The Need to Find Order in a Confusing World." *Psychology Today* (January 6, 2018), https://www.psychologytoday.com/us/blog/talking-apes/201801/why-do-people-believe-in-conspiracy-theories.

Lusthaus, Jonathan. "A History of Hell: The Jewish Origins of the Idea of *Gehenna* in the Gospels of Matthew and Mark." *Australian Religion Studies Review* 21.2 (2008): 175-187.

Maier, Harry O. *Apocalypse Recalled: the Book of Revelation after Christendom*. Minneapolis: Fortress Press, 2002.

Mark, Joshua J. "Gilgamesh." *Ancient History Encyclopedia* (2018): https://www.ancient.eu/gilgamesh/.

Methodius of Olympus, *From the Discourse on the Resurrection*. In *Fathers of the Third Century*. Ante-Nicene Fathers, Vol. 6. Edin-

burgh: T&T Clark, 1885. https://ccel.org/ccel/methodius
/resurrection/anf06.

Middleton, J. Richard. "A New Heaven and a New Earth: The Case
for a Holistic Reading of the Biblical Story of Redemption."
Journal for Christian Theological Research 11 (2006): 73-97.
http://www2.luthersem.edu/ctrf/JCTR/Vol11/Middleton_
vol11.pdf.

———. *A New Heaven and a New Earth: Reclaiming Biblical Eschatology.*
Grand Rapids: Baker Academic, 2014.

Moore, David George. *The Battle for Hell: A Survey and Evaluation of
Evangelicals' Growing Attraction to the Doctrine of Annihilationism.*
New York: University Press of America, Inc., 1995.

Muratorian Fragment. Translated by Bruce M. Metzger. http://www
.earlychristianwritings.com/text/muratorian-metzger.html.

Murphy, Frederick James. *Apocalypticism in the Bible and Its World:
A Comprehensive Introduction.* Grand Rapids: Baker Academic,
2012.

Noble, Thomas A. "The Mission of the Holy Trinity." In *Missio Dei: A
Wesleyan Understanding.* Edited by Keith Schwanz and Joseph
Coleson. Kansas City, MO: Beacon Hill Press of Kansas City,
2011.

Norris, Richard A. "Theology and Language in Irenaeus of Lyon." In
Recent Studies in Early Christianity: a Collection of Scholarly Essays.
Ed. by Everett Ferguson. New York: Garland Publishing, Inc.,
1999.

O'Day, Gail R. "The Gospel of John," 491-865. In *The New Interpreter's Bible*, Vol. 9. Nashville: Abingdon Press, 1995.

Papaioannou, Kim. "Motifs of Death and Hell in the Teaching of
Jesus: Part 1—An Examination of Hades." *Melanesia Journal of
Theology* 32.2 (2016): 103-133.

———. "Motifs of Death and Hell in the Teaching of Jesus, Part 2:
An Examination of Gehenna," *Melanesian Journal of Theology*
33.1–2 (2017): 7-32.

Peterson, Brent D. "What Is the Point of God's Mission?" In *Missio
Dei: A Wesleyan Understanding.* Edited by Keith Schwanz and
Joseph Coleson. Kansas City, MO: Beacon Hill Press of Kansas
City, 2011.

Rossing, Barbara R. *The Rapture Exposed: The Message of Hope in the
Book of Revelation.* New York: Basic Books, 2005.

"*Saeculum.*" In *Oxford Latin Dictionary.* Ed. by P. G. W. Glare. New
York: Oxford University Press, 1982.

Sasse, Hermann. "Αἰών, αἰώνιος." *Theological Dictionary of the New Testament*, Vol. 1. Edited by G. Kittel, G. W. Bromiley, & G. Friedrich. Grand Rapids: Eerdmans, 1977.

Schmemann, Alexander. *For the Life of the World*. Crestwood, NY: St. Vladimir's Seminary Press, 1963.

Snyder, Howard A., and Joel Scandrett. *Salvation Means Creation Healed: The Ecology of Sin and Grace: Overcoming the Divorce between Earth and Heaven*. Eugene, OR: Cascade Books, 2011.

Tertullian. *Prescription Against Heretics*. In *Latin Christianity: Its Founder, Tertullian*. Ante-Nicene Fathers, Vol. 3. Edinburgh: T&T Clark, 1885. https://ccel.org/ccel/tertullian/heretics/anf03.

Thompson, J. A. *The Book of Jeremiah*. The New International Commentary on the Old Testament. Grand Rapids: Eerdmans, 1980.

Tsumura, David Toshio. *Creation and Destruction: A Reappraisal of the Chaoskampf Theory in the Old Testament*. Winona Lake, IN: Eisenbrauns, 2005.

Vail, Eric M. *Atonement and Salvation: The Extravagance of God's Love*. Kansas City, MO: Beacon Hill Press of Kansas City, 2016.

―――. "Creation out of Nothing Remodeled." In *Theologies of Creation: Creatio ex Nihilo and Its New Rivals*. Edited by Thomas Jay Oord. New York: Routledge, 2015.

―――. "The Holiness Foundation of Mission." *Didache: Faithful Teaching* 13:1 (Summer 2013): http://didache.nazarene.org/index.php/volume-13-1/894-didache-v13n1-03-mission-vail1/file, 1.

Vincent of Lérins. *A Commonitory*. In *Fathers of the Second Century*. Ante-Nicene Fathers, Vol. 2. Edinburgh: T&T Clark, 1885. http://www.ccel.org/ccel/schaff/npnf211.iii.iii.html.

Walton, John H. *The Lost World of Genesis One: Ancient Cosmology and the Origins Debate*. Downers Grove, IL: InterVarsity Press, 2009.

Watson, Duane F. "Death, Second." In *The Anchor Bible Dictionary: Vol. 2*. New York: Doubleday, 1992.

Weber, Timothy. "Dispensational Premillennialism: The Dispensationalist Era." *Christian History Institute* 61 (1999): https://christianhistoryinstitute.org/magazine/article/dispensational-premillennialism-the-dispensationalist-era/.

Wenham, Gordon J. "Sanctuary Symbolism in the Garden of Eden Story," 399–404. In *I Studied Inscriptions from before the Flood: Ancient Near Eastern, Literary, and Linguistic Approaches to Gen-*

esis 1–11. *Sources for Biblical and Theological Study*, Vol. 4. Ed. by Hess and Tsumura. Winona Lake, IN: Eisenbrauns, 1994.

Wright, N. T. *Surprised by Hope: Rethinking Heaven, the Resurrection, and the Mission of the Church.* New York: HarperOne, 2008.

Ziegler, Philip G. *Militant Grace: The Apocalyptic Turn and the Future of Christian Theology.* Grand Rapids: Baker Academic, 2018.

Recommended Resources

Historical Sources on Resurrection (by year)

Justin Martyr (AD 100-165), "On the Resurrection," Chapters 2-5, 7-10. http://www.ccel.org/ccel/schaff/anf01.viii.viii.ii.html.

Irenaeus (AD 130-202), *Against Heresies*, Book 2, Chapter 34.3-4. http://www.ccel.org/ccel/schaff/anf01.ix.iii.xxxv.html.

———, *Against Heresies*, Book 3, Ch 16. http://www.ccel.org/ccel/schaff/anf01.ix.iv.xvii.html.

———, *Against Heresies*, Book 5, Chapters 9, 10, and 11. http://www.ccel.org/ccel/schaff/anf01.ix.vii.x.html.

Methodius of Olympus (AD 250-311), "From the Discourse on the Resurrection," Part I, Paragraphs VI-XIII. http://www.ccel.org/ccel/schaff/anf06.xi.v.i.html.

Origen (d. AD 254), *On First Principles* (*De Principiis*), Book 3, Chapter 6. http://www.ccel.org/ccel/schaff/anf04.vi.v.iv.viii.html.

Chrysostom (AD 347-407), *Homilies on First Corinthians*, Homilies 39, 40, 41, 42. http://www.ccel.org/ccel/schaff/npnf112.iv.xl.html.

Augustine (AD 354-430), *City of God*, Book 13, Chapters 20, 22, 23. http://www.ccel.org/ccel/schaff/npnf102.iv.XIII.20.html.

———, *City of God*, Book 22, Chapters 21, 29, 30. http://www.ccel.org/ccel/schaff/npnf102.iv.XXII.21.html.

John Wesley (AD 1703-1791), "On the Resurrection of the Dead." http://wesley.nnu.edu/john-wesley/the-sermons-of-john-wesley-1872-edition/sermon-137-on-the-resurrection-of-the-dead/.

On Sheol, Hades, and Gehenna

Duke, Rodney K. "Eternal Torment or Destruction? Interpreting Final Judgment Texts." *Evangelical Quarterly* 88.3 (2016/17): 237-258.

Papaioannou, Kim. "Motifs of Death and Hell in the Teaching of Jesus: Part 1—An Examination of Hades." *Melanesia Journal of Theology* 32.2 (2016): 103-133.

———. "Motifs of Death and Hell in the Teaching of Jesus, Part 2: An Examination of Gehenna," *Melanesian Journal of Theology* 33.1–2 (2017): 7-32.

On New Creation and the Big Picture

Middleton, J. Richard. "A New Heaven and a New Earth: The Case for a Holistic Reading of the Biblical Story of Redemption." *Journal for Christian Theological Research* 11 (2006): 73-97. http://www2.luthersem.edu/ctrf/JCTR/Vol11/Middleton_vol11.pdf.

———. *A New Heaven and a New Earth: Reclaiming Biblical Eschatology.* Grand Rapids: Baker Academic, 2014.

Snyder, Howard A., and Joel Scandrett. *Salvation Means Creation Healed: The Ecology of Sin and Grace: Overcoming the Divorce between Earth and Heaven.* Eugene, OR: Cascade Books, 2011.

Wright, N. T. *Surprised by Hope: Rethinking Heaven, the Resurrection, and the Mission of the Church.* New York: HarperOne, 2008.

On the Book of Revelation

General Audience

Boone, Dan. *Answers for Chicken Little: A No-Nonsense Look at the Book of Revelation.* Kansas City, MO: Beacon Hill Press of Kansas City, 2005.

Daniels, Scott. *Seven Deadly Spirits: The Message of Revelation's Letters for Today's Church.* Grand Rapids: Baker Academic, 2009.

DeSilva, David A. *Unholy Allegiances: Heeding Revelation's Warning.* Peabody, MA: Hendrickson Publishers, 2013.

Gorman, Michael J. *Reading Revelation Responsibly: Uncivil Worship and Witness: Following the Lamb into the New Creation.* Eugene, OR: Cascade Books, 2011.

Rossing, Barbara R. *The Rapture Exposed: The Message of Hope in the Book of Revelation.* New York: Basic Books, 2005.

Informed Audience

Bauckham, Richard. *The Theology of the Book of Revelation.* Cambridge: Cambridge University Press, 1993.

Hansen, Ryan L. *Silence and Praise: Rhetorical Cosmology and Political Theology in the Book of Revelation.* Minneapolis: Fortress Press, 2014.

Rotz, Carol. *Revelation: A Commentary in the Wesleyan Tradition.* New Beacon Bible Commentary (Kansas City, MO: Beacon Hill Press of Kansas City, 2012).

Video Resources

Boyd, Greg. *Rescuing Revelation: Sermon Series.* https://whchurch.org
/sermon_series/rescuing-revelation.

Parry, Robin. "'Hell' or Sheol, Hades, Gehenna, and Tartarus?" (0:00
– 7:46). https://youtu.be/Q8oimqS0DsY.

Rossing, Barbara. "Apocalypse Now: Revelation so the World is not
'Left Behind,'" (20:55 - 55:04). https://youtu.be/5V4lkH6TsR4

Witherington III, Ben. "Where Did Rapture Theology Come From?"
(0:00 – 5:55). https://www.youtube.com/watch?v=d_cVXdr8m-
Vs.

Wright, N. T. "Discerning the Dawn: Knowing God in the New Creation," (0:00 – 57:00). https://youtu.be/ZGX4EcJFupQ.

———. "Going to Heaven is NOT the Christian Hope," (0:00 –
6:12). https://youtu.be/NE_-5zJCOEs.

———. "History, Eschatology and New Creation" (2:40 – 36:45).
https://www.youtube.com/watch?v=yf2SJb55iJ0.

———. "How God Became King: Why We've All Misunderstood
the Gospels," (5:40 – 1:00:25). https://www.youtube.com/
watch?v=Mks4gYcjpXc.

———. "N. T. Wright on Rapture," (0:00 – 5:30). https://www
.youtube.com/watch?v=iqYHeBdMqvU.

———. "NT Wright answers Questions about Heaven, Hell, & Resurrection." *100huntley* (2008): videos 1-14 https://
www.youtube.com/watch?v=W0Dc01HVlaM&list=PLD966
D6224EA97F83.

———. "Resurrection and the Renewal of Creation," (0:00 -
1:04:00). https://youtu.be/GenlGUkZ-6Q.

———. "Revelation and Christian Hope: Political Implications of
the Revelation to John," (0:00 – 53:50). https://www.you
tube.com/watch?v=YW-7baAbaVM.

———. "The Kingdom of Heaven will be ON Earth," (0:00 – 2:10).
https://youtu.be/UIdboWSQcDQ.